GCSE IN A WEEK
AUTHOR – SEAN O'BYRNE

Use this day-by-day listing and the tabs on each page in the book to plan your revision.

COMPUTER SYSTEMS

What is a computer?

> A computer is an electronic, high speed, programmable data processing device.

- Computers are built from solid-state electronic components, and that's why they are fast.

- They don't make mistakes – they do exactly what they are told.

- Most computers are **general purpose**. They can do different jobs depending on what programs they are running.

- Some computers are **dedicated** to a single purpose. These include the **embedded systems** that control devices such as digital cameras and DVD players.

What are computers good at?

A job is suitable for a computer if any of these are important:

Reason	Example
Accuracy is essential.	The wrong amount on an invoice could cost a company money.
Speed is essential.	The travel agent needs to know now whether a holiday is available.
Information is needed in various different forms.	A garage owner needs the service history of a car and a report on all services carried out this month.
The job is repetitive and boring.	Thousands of cheques are processed every day.
It is dangerous or inconvenient for a person to do the job.	A robot is investigating a suspect package.
There aren't enough people available to do the job or people are too expensive.	You wouldn't employ a separate person to control each set of traffic lights in a city.

Data, information and knowledge

- Computers work with **data**. Data is a collection of facts or figures. Computers don't understand data, they just process it. Data could be something like 121297. A computer can be programmed to do anything to this data, such as add a number to it.

- People prefer to work with **information**. Information is data in context. It has added meaning. If the number 121297 is expressed as 12/12/97, we know it is a date.

- Knowledge is understanding information and knowing what can be done with it.

- Computers can **combine** data. Software can be used to quickly build up a profile of a criminal by combining the locations and characteristics of lots of crimes.

- Computers can quickly **search** for data. Some police cars are now fitted with a system that, given a number plate, can immediately report if a car is stolen.

Progress check

1 Which of these jobs are suitable for a computer?
   a) Writing a note to the milkman.
   b) Controlling the flight path of an aircraft.
   c) Deciding what new products a company should launch.
   d) Processing millions of exam marks.
   e) Predicting tomorrow's weather.
   f) Deciding on the right treatment for a sick patient.

2 What is a small computer called that controls a larger device such as a microwave oven?

3 What is a dedicated computer system?

4 Fill in the gaps.
   Computers process ...., but people prefer working with
   ....
   Computers can do lots of different things because you can
   .... them.

DAY
1
2
3
4
5
6
7

TYPES OF COMPUTER

Microcomputers

- The most common computers are microcomputers – small computers. However, computers used to be huge.

- Nearly all microcomputers are personal computers (PCs).

Desktop PCs

Desktop PCs are the machines that most people think of as computers. Most businesses and many homes have them. Each PC has:

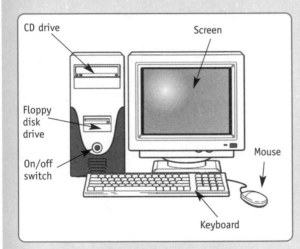

Networked PCs

PCs are often networked so that the users can **communicate** and **share resources** such as printers.

Laptop PCs

Laptop PCs are small portable PCs. Some extremely small ones are called **notebooks**. Laptops are suitable for working:

- while travelling (e.g. on a train)
- when you need to move from one room to another (e.g. while teaching or visiting various offices)
- when working outside (e.g. checking and starting Formula 1 cars on the grid)

Many laptops have access to the Internet or a network by radio. This can be a security problem.

Mini and mainframe computers

These big computers are usually owned by large organisations. They often provide central processing for lots of connected **terminals**.

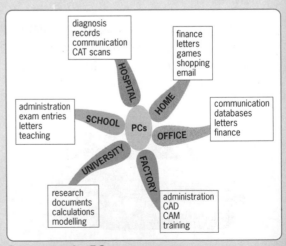

Some uses for PCs

Computers come in various shapes and sizes. They are good at different things.

Personal digital assistants (PDAs)

PDAs are popular for taking brief notes while travelling. They are small enough to hold in the hand, but do not have proper, full-size keyboards.

Embedded systems

Many electronic devices contain dedicated computer systems. They have a processor and software stored in a ROM chip. They are found in:

- cameras – to work out the correct exposure

- videos – to control timed recordings

- washing machines – to manage the wash cycles

- car engine management systems – to increase fuel efficiency

- DVD and CD players – to decode the signals

Progress check

1 Give two uses for a PC in the home.

2 Give two uses for a PC in a school.

3 What is a PDA?

4 What is a computer connected to a mainframe called?

5 What is the difference between a desktop PC and a laptop PC?

6 Give one reason why digital cameras contain embedded systems.

DAY
1

The need for storage

The RAM of a computer loses its data when the power is switched off. Any data that is needed in the future must be **saved** if it is to be used again.

Magnetic storage

Magnetic disks come in two main types:

Floppy disks store a small amount of data – 1.44 Mb. They are useful for:

- backing up small files
- moving data between computers

However, they are slow and often unreliable.

Most computers have at least one **hard disk** installed. They store:

- the application programs
- the operating system
- data

Magnetic strips

These are found on cards such as credit and debit cards, and also on travel tickets and sometimes car park tickets. They do not hold much data.

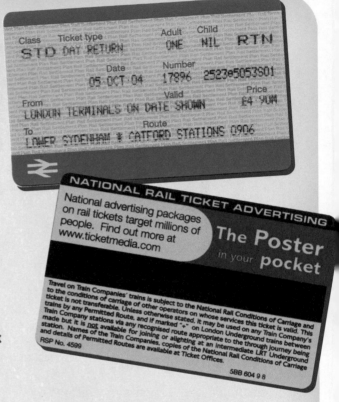

Electronic storage

Data is often stored on electronic chips. Examples are:

- programs on ROM chips in embedded systems
- data on smart cards such as viewing permissions on digital TV systems
- backup data on memory sticks – these plug into the USB port and can store large amounts of data
- image files on camera memory chips
- music on portable digital players

○ Optical storage

Optical storage is used by CDs and DVDs (digital versatile disks). They are plastic disks written to and read by **laser** beams.

- They are very reliable.
- They hold huge amounts of data.
- They are compatible with other electronic systems such as DVD and CD music players.

Optical storage is suitable for:

- backing up lots of data
- archiving data (keeping old records in case they are needed)
- multimedia presentations such as encyclopaedias
- distributing software
- music files (mostly CDs)
- movies (DVDs)

Progress check

Fill in the gaps.

1 A plastic card with an embedded chip that stores data is called a

....

2 Two uses for a CD are

.... and

....

3 Movies are stored digitally on optical disks called ....

4 New software is distributed on

....

5 Floppy disks are suitable for

.... and

....

DAY 1

All computer systems take in data, do something to it and give back a result.

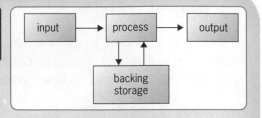

input → process → output

process ↔ backing storage

Hardware and software

Hardware – the **physical** bits and pieces of a computer system. This ranges from devices such as printers to cables, chips and plugs.

Software – the **programs** that contain the instructions to the hardware telling it what to do.

Software comes in two main types:

● **operating systems** – control the hardware

● **applications** – do useful jobs for us

The processor unit

Most computers have a processor unit. This is a box that contains:

Part	Description
A motherboard	A framework for plugging in and connecting the components.
Other circuit boards	There may be separate boards for sound or video output or for network connection.
Buses	Sets of wires that carry data and signals between the parts.
The processor itself	Carries out the program instructions.
Memory	Where data and instructions are stored while in use.
Device controllers	Circuit boards that give instructions to disk drives and other devices.
A power supply	Reduces voltage of mains supply and converts AC to DC.
At least one hard disk drive	More can be added.
Various other drives	May include floppy, CD, CDRW and DVD drives.
Ports	Sockets that allow the connection of other devices.

Most computer systems are made up of similar parts. They are for input, processing and output.

Peripherals

These are devices that are connected to the processor unit. They include input and output devices such as keyboards and printers. Some peripherals, such as a modem, can be both input and output.

Peripherals also include the hardware that goes to make up a network such as hubs, switches and routers.

Other types of computer

Other types of computer also have hardware, software and storage. A washing machine controller is on a **hardware** chip and it has **control software** that is **stored** in its ROM.

Progress check

Fill in the gaps.

1. The processor, memory and a printer are all examples of ....

2. Software comes in two main types: .... and ....

3. The parts in a computer's processor unit communicate via ....

4. Software consists of ...., which tell the processor what to do.

5. Any hardware connected to the processor unit is called a ....

6. The software that controls a household appliance such as a washing machine is stored in its ....

7. An example of a device that is both input and output is a ....

8. A computer's power supply unit .... the mains voltage.

DAY 1

Memory

Memory is where **data** and **program instructions** are stored.

- It is divided into millions of 'boxes' called **locations**.
- All memory locations are the same size. They each hold one byte of data.
- One byte is made from eight bits.

The bits are either on or off. The meaning of this bit pattern depends on its location. Some locations are designated data and some are instructions. The meaning of each part is decided on by the software.

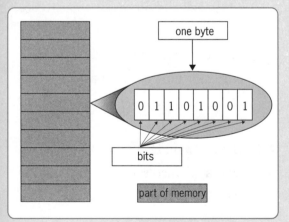

All data entering and leaving a computer must pass through memory.

> **When data is stored in memory, it is written. When data is copied from memory, it is read.**

Two types of memory

Random Access Memory or RAM

- It is called Random Access because data can be written to or read from any location.
- Most memory is RAM. A PC might have 256 Mb of RAM, which is more than 256 million locations.
- RAM **loses** its data when the power is switched off.
- Programs have to be copied into RAM before they can run.

Read-Only Memory or ROM

- ROM can only be read. Its contents are stored there during manufacture.
- There is not much ROM in most computers.
- ROM **keeps** its data when switched off.
- ROM contains basic start-up instructions and these are run when a computer is switched on.
- In many devices, such as washing machines, ROM is used to store the program instructions because they don't need to be changed.

The processor

This does all the work on the data. It is built on a silicon chip. It is sometimes called a **microprocessor** because it is very small.

- It gets the instructions from memory – one at a time.
- It carries out the program instructions.
- It performs calculations.
- It compares items of data.
- It moves data from one place to another.

The processor is connected to memory by wires called **buses**. The processor is made from many **logic circuits**. Logic circuits contain components called **logic gates**.

- AND gates give out a signal when they receive two signals at once.
- OR gates give out a signal if they receive one or two signals.
- NOT gates reverse the one signal they receive, so 0 becomes 1 and 1 becomes 0.

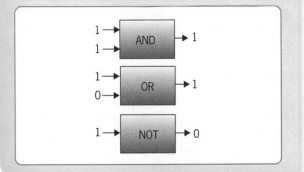

Progress check

1 Name two things that are stored in RAM.

2 Which type of memory loses its data when the power is switched off?

3 What is ROM used for?

4 Describe two jobs of the processor.

5 An OR gate receives one input signal. What is the output?

6 An AND gate receives one input signal. What is the output?

COMPUTER INPUT

> Input is the data that is fed into a computer system.
> The computer then processes this data according to its
> program instructions and gives back the results as output.

There are many types of input. There are input devices designed for each type.

Manual methods

There are three manual methods of input.

Method	Used for
QWERTY keyboard	text
Mouse	selecting items
Touch-sensitive screen and concept keyboards	selecting items

Direct entry

These quick methods can reduce the number of mistakes made.

Method	How it works	Example
OMR (optical mark recognition)	Pencil marks on a sheet are read in by machine.	Lottery entry
OCR (optical character recognition)	Text is read by machine.	Postcodes on letters
MICR (magnetic ink character recognition)	Special ink is used, so fraudulent changes are not registered by the system.	Cheques
Barcodes	A pattern of lines is scanned.	Items in a shop, books
Magnetic strip	A small amount of data is stored in the strip on a card.	Older credit cards, train and underground tickets
Smart cards	A chip is embedded in a card with data stored in it.	Credit cards, digital TV viewing box

Sensors

These convert physical events into electronic signals.

Used in	Examples
Scientific experiments	pH, temperature, electric current and pressure
Weather recording	Hours of sunshine, rainfall and humidity
Process control	Flow rate, temperature, concentration
Engine management	Temperatures, fuel consumption, engine speed

Many sensors record analogue data, whereas computers use digital data. This means that sensors often have to be connected to a computer via an analogue–digital converter.

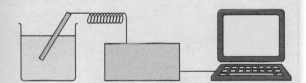

Progress check

1. What type of device would be used to do the following?
   a) check tyre pressures in a racing car
   b) monitor the rate of chemical usage in a manufacturing process
   c) input the customer names of those who have sent in orders
   d) choose an option in application software

2. What device needs to be connected between most physical sensors and a computer?

3. What is MICR?

4. How does MICR reduce fraud?

Fill in the gaps.

5. A teacher records the attendance register by making marks on a machine-readable form. This is called ....

6. Goods are identified at a supermarket checkout by reading their ....

DAY 1

Just as computers can receive signals as input, they can produce other signals as output. These signals can be displayed or they can drive other devices.

○ Screen display

Screen display is used for temporary display or when movement is important. Sometimes a screen is called a visual display unit (VDU).

Display type	Comments
Cathode ray tube (CRT) monitor	The most common type of display – cheap, heavy and gets hot.
Flat screen monitor, usually thin film transistor (TFT) screens which are a type of liquid crystal display (LCD)	Increasingly popular as the price comes down and quality improves. Laptops have these.

○ Projectors

Computers can be connected to data projectors. These produce large images for a public display and are useful for presentations. For teaching, they may be combined with an interactive whiteboard.

○ Printers

Printers are needed when hard copy is required.

Type	Used for	How it works
Laser	High quality output – good for large quantities.	Toner powder is attracted to paper by electrostatic charge, and then fused on by hot roller.
Ink jet	Quality output so suitable for small quantities or home use. Ink is expensive.	Ink is heated in cartridge and sprayed onto the paper.
Dot matrix	Bills and credit card vouchers – useful where self-copying paper is needed.	Letters are formed by **impact** of pins, making an image by striking inked ribbon.

Computers exist to produce output. Output can be in many forms.

○ Plotters

These make **line drawings** by moving a pen over a sheet of paper. They are used by designers and architects.

○ Actuators

These are any devices that make things happen, such as:

- **motors** that can be controlled by computer signals for all sorts of purposes from moving the flaps on an aircraft to opening greenhouse windows

- **solenoids** that control valves in industrial or chemical processes

- **lights** such as traffic lights, that can be controlled by computers

- **heaters** that can be computer-controlled in greenhouses, washing machines and ovens

○ Sound

Two examples of sound output devices are:

- **speakers** are used to play music and speech or just to make noises to alert the user that something has happened

- **sirens** can be the sound output from a burglar alarm system

Progress check

1 What type of printer is suitable for long print runs of high quality?

2 Why might dot matrix printers be used for printing credit card vouchers?

3 What type of output device is needed to show a moving image?

4 What special output device makes hard copy line drawings of a design?

5 What type of display device does a laptop computer have?

6 What output devices could be used to help control the temperature in a greenhouse?

DAY **2**

Devices and media

Media are the materials that store data such as disks and tapes. **Devices** are the hardware items that write data onto the media or read it back.

Magnetic tapes

- Tapes are long, thin, magnetic media.
- They can store huge amounts of data.
- It is slow to find data on a tape because it has to be wound to the right position before the data is read.
- Tapes are used for storing backup data, especially on networks, and big files for mainframe computers.

Disks

Disks can hold random access files, which makes them good for searching and quickly updating files. Interactive applications such as booking systems need to use disks so that updates are stored immediately.

Magnetic disks

With both floppy and hard disks, data is stored in the same way. Parts of the surface can be magnetised in one direction or another. This allows the storage of 0s and 1s. The difference is that hard disks:

- store much more data
- are accessed much more quickly
- are generally not transportable
- are usually made from a set of disks called **platters**

Optical storage

CDs and DVDs can hold a lot of data. DVDs hold more than CDs. Data is stored on them by making small pits in the surface of a membrane by a laser beam. The pits are arranged in a spiral. A laser also reads the data back.

Magnetic disks are **written to** and **read from** by a **read-write head** in the disk drive. It moves in and out to reach each track. Optical disks need a laser to write and read back the data.

Magnetic disks need to be **formatted** before they can be used. This is like painting lines in a car park – the location of the data is set out. Most disks are formatted before being sold.

Finding data on a disk

One track on a disk contains the disk directory or **file allocation table** (FAT). It stores the location of the files on the disk. The operating system of the computer uses this directory to tell the read-write mechanism to go to the correct track.

Tracks, sectors and cylinders

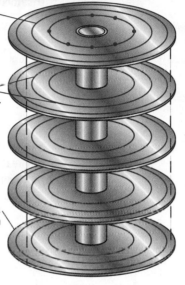

A **track** is one complete circle on a disk.

A **sector** Is part of a track. A sector contains a **block** of data that is read or written in one operation.

A **cylinder** is a set of tracks in the same position on each platter of a disk pack.

Fragmentation

When a file is deleted from a disk, the space that it occupied can be used again. If it is not big enough for the next file to be saved, the file will be broken up and spread across available sectors. A file like this is **fragmented**. It is slower to read broken up files. From time to time, it may be worth **defragmenting** a disk. Defragmenting is getting the operating system to move the parts of the files together in order to speed up performance.

Progress check

Fill in the gaps.

1 Before a floppy disk can be used for the first time, it must be

....

2 On magnetic disks, data is stored in circular paths called ....

3 Each circle of data is divided into a number of ....

4 Tapes cannot hold .... files, but disks can.

5 The operating system finds files on disks by looking up their location in the ....

6 The data on CDs and DVDs is read by directing a .... at the disk.

7 A file that is broken up across different disk locations is

....

8 A platter is part of a ....

DAY 2

Automatic data entry is much **quicker** and much more **reliable** than having people type it in.

Method	How it works	Example	Advantages	Disadvantages
OMR (optical mark recognition)	Pen or pencil marks on a special form.	Lottery choices	No special equipment needed to enter data.	Badly placed marks or crumpled forms are not read properly.
OCR (optical character recognition)	Printed words are read by machine.	Postcodes on envelopes	Readable by people and machines.	Some fonts and handwriting are not read properly.
MICR (magnetic ink character recognition)	Special characters printed in magnetic ink.	Numbers on cheques	Difficult to forge changes.	Expensive, special equipment needed to read.
Barcode	Pattern of thin and thick lines read by scanner or wand. Identifies an item.	Items in shops, books, parcels	Very quick data entry.	Dirty barcodes are not read.
Magnetic strip	Magnetised strip on back of a card. Same technology as magnetic disks.	Older credit cards, car parking tickets, travel tickets	Quick to read, so useful at automatic ticket barriers.	Holds little data and can be forged.
Smart cards	Computer chip embedded in card.	Credit cards, TV viewing cards, identity cards	Lots of data can be stored and changed. Takes little space.	Sometimes a reading machine is not available, e.g. small traders may not be able to verify a credit card.

There are lots of ways to capture data automatically. Exams often ask about these.

20 MINS

Automatic methods are useful in security systems. Some use **biometrics**. This is where some physical characteristic of a person is recognised such as:

- a fingerprint
- the pattern of blood vessels on the retina
- face shape

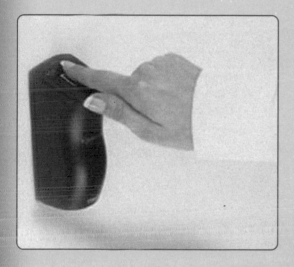

My credit card is read by a machine.

The magnetic strip on my plane ticket is checked.

DEPARTURES

The bar code on my luggage is scanned.

Networks are computers and other devices that are linked together.

ADVANTAGES OF NETWORKS

Communications
Messages and files can be sent from one computer to others.

Flexibility
It doesn't matter which computer you use if they can all access the same resources.

File sharing
Many people can work on the same data.

Software sharing
If software is installed centrally, it is easier to upgrade.

Peripheral sharing
Expensive peripherals, such as colour laser printers, can be shared.

DISADVANTAGES OF NETWORKS

Skills
It takes a lot of expertise to set up and maintain a big network.

Security
This includes passwords, data encryption and user groups and permissions.

Viruses
They can spread quickly on a network.

Expense
The expertise and network software licences can be expensive.

Reliability
If a network has problems, lots of people might be affected.

Types of network

- A **LAN** (Local Area Network) is a network located at one site.
- A **WAN** (Wide Area Network) is a network that covers a large geographical area.

Client-server

Most networks have at least one **server**. This stores files centrally and coordinates network activity.

The **workstations** that connect to the servers are called **clients**. Peer-to-peer networks have no server.

Topology

Most networks are either **bus**, **star** or **ring**. Star networks are the most reliable.

Protocols

The rules for devices communicating are called protocols. The most common set of protocols is TCP/IP (transmission control protocol/Internet protocol).

Linking devices

- Most networks are linked by cable or radio.
- Each device on a network is connected to it by a network interface card (NIC).

Progress check

A doctor's surgery has five computers, one in each consulting room and one at reception. The doctors want to network the computers.

1. What would be the cheapest topology to use?

2. Give three advantages of networking the computers.

3. What worries might patients have over networking the computers?

4. What ongoing costs will the doctors face with their network?

5. What hardware must every device on the network have?

OPERATING SYSTEMS

Operating systems are software. They control the hardware of the computer and its peripherals. They make it possible for people and applications to communicate with the hardware. Networks require special operating systems.

Windows
This is the most widespread, graphics-based operating system on PCs and it is owned by Microsoft.

Unix
Extremely popular on larger, more powerful systems. Character-based, but graphic shells available. A smaller system than Windows.

Linux
An 'open source' version of Unix. The source code is in the public domain and is not 'owned' by anybody. Popular on web servers.

Multitasking
Most modern operating systems allow more than one program to be in memory at the same time. They then share out processor time between the programs.

⬭ Interfaces

Operating systems provide interfaces: that is a connection between the hardware and the user or another program.

Graphic user interface (GUI)

The screen displays bit-mapped graphics. This includes **icons,** which are pictures that represent programs or other resources.

⬇

Easy to use (no commands need to be learned).

⬇

Designed to be operated by mouse action.

⬇

Requires a lot of memory (bit-mapped graphics tend to be big files).

⬇

Requires a lot of processing power (a lot of pictures need to be redrawn when they move).

⬇

Provides settings so that the user can customise the machine.

Command line interface (CLI)

Requires commands to be typed in.

⬇

Requires commands to be learned.

⬇

Uses less memory than GUIs.

⬇

Runs quicker and need less processing.

⬇

Lets the user batch commands to customise the machine.

Operating systems control the hardware. You need to be able to remember some of the specific jobs they do.

Menu driven interfaces

These allow the user to choose from a set of options. A good example is the interface of some bank cash machines.

◯ Other operating system jobs

- Finding space on disks to save files.
- Providing a filing system of folders (directories).
- Finding space in memory for a program.
- Scheduling tasks – allocating processor time to each program.
- Controlling the security of files.

Drivers: Drivers are programs that allow a computer to communicate with devices.

Utilities: Operating systems come with lots of handy tools for customising the computer, such as a media player and a disk defragmenter.

The registry: Windows stores details of the programs on a computer's hard disk in files called the **registry**.

Progress check

1. What type of interface is controlled by mouse actions?

2. Describe two utilities often provided with operating systems.

3. What software is used by an operating system to communicate with a peripheral device?

4. Give one example of how an operating system can provide security for important files.

5. What is a multitasking operating system?

DAY 2

What are applications?

An application is software that is designed to do a useful job. There are thousands of examples. Applications are **problem-oriented**, whereas operating systems are **machine-oriented**.

Generic applications

These are examples of common applications:

- word processors
- spreadsheets
- database management systems
- payroll systems
- booking systems

Generic applications are off-the-shelf. They have been written for the mass market. This usually means they are:

- available straight away
- economical to buy
- well tested
- well supported by books and websites

Some of these can be customised to make new applications. For example, a spreadsheet can be set up to calculate and print invoices.

Specially-written applications

Much software is designed for one particular job, such as:

- a control system in an industrial process
- a guidance system for a missile
- a computer game

- an exam results processing system

Specially-written software is more expensive and takes longer to get ready, but it should be:

- designed especially for a user's requirements
- supported by individual training
- upgradable according to the customer's wishes

Database management systems

Many business applications are based on database management systems. Like spreadsheets, they can be considered as **application generators** because a wide range of specialised applications can be created from them.

Applications are the reason why people buy computers. You must be aware of a wide range of applications.

Microsoft Access is a good example of a database management system, but there are more powerful ones available.

Database management systems can be used to make many different useful applications. Examples are:

- stock control systems
- booking systems
- inventories
- personnel record systems
- timetabling systems

Database management systems allow the separation of the data from the applications.

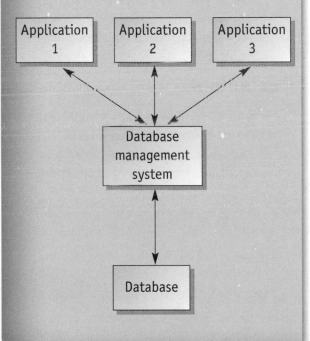

Progress check

1. Here are some jobs that a computer can perform. Which are jobs for the operating system and which are for applications?

   a) finding space in memory for a program
   b) controlling traffic lights
   c) printing payslips
   d) booking a holiday
   e) saving a file to disk
   f) controlling a printer
   g) navigating an aircraft

2. What is the difference between a database and a database management system?

SPREADSHEETS

● Cells

Spreadsheets are made from a grid of **cells**. These cells can hold various types of data as well as formulae and functions which do things. The cells are arranged in rows and columns.

● Addresses

Each cell has an **address** or **coordinates**. The columns are designated with letters and the rows with numbers, so cell A1 is the top right cell.

● Naming cells

If you want to refer to a cell, you can give it a name instead of trying to remember its coordinate.

● Absolute cell addressing

When you copy a cell that contains a formula, the references change with it. If you don't want this to happen, you can fix the reference by using dollar signs. A12 refers to cell A12 but it won't change if it is copied.

● Data types

Spreadsheets can recognise several different data types.

● **Text:** if there are any letters or other characters, the cell is treated as text. Text is left-aligned by default.

● **Numbers:** if a cell contains just numbers (and maybe a decimal point), the entry is treated as a number and calculations can be done on it.

● **Dates:** if you enter a date in a standard way, such as 23/11/77, this is recognised as a date and is converted into a day number. It is stored as this number but displayed as a date. Dates can be added and subtracted.

● Autofill

There are easy ways to copy a value, a formula or a function across a range of cells. This can be done by keyboard or mouse action. This is called **replication**.

● Formulae and functions

Formulae can be written to do calculations. For example, =A12*A13 means multiply the contents of cells A12 and A13.

Functions are pre-written instructions that can be called by name. They have **arguments**, which are the data that they are to work with placed in brackets. For example, =SUM(A1:A10) means add up all the values in the cell range A1 to A10.

Charts and graphs

Spreadsheets can make lots of different types of graph. This is useful for summarising data.

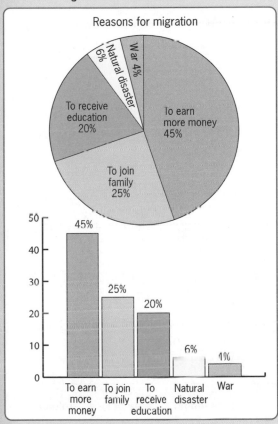

Reasons for migration

Spreadsheets as databases

Spreadsheets can be used to set up simple **flat file** databases. They can store data in rows (records) and columns (fields).

The data can be:

- sorted
- filtered, to show just some of the data.

Progress check

Here is part of a spreadsheet.

	A	B	C	D	E	F
1	Surname	Forename	Paper 1	Paper 2	Paper 3	Total Mark
2	King	Greg	54	36	67	157
3	Smith	Jack	45	34	76	155
4	French	Mary	23	43	22	88
5	Kaur	Parminder	54	43	34	131
6						

1 Identify a cell that contains

    a) text data

    b) numeric data

    c) a function

2 Which cells could have had data entered by autofill?

3 Which cells would have to be high-lighted before the data could be put into alphabetical order by name?

4 The average mark for Paper 1 is required in cell C6. What formula would have to be made in that cell?

5 The average marks are also required for Papers 2 and 3. What is the quickest way to achieve this?

DAY

3

MODELLING

What is a model?

A model is a set of mathematical relationships. It is produced to help make predictions of real-world events. Models are useful in lots of situations.

Reason	Example
The event is in the future.	Tomorrow's weather
The event is dangerous.	Testing car air bags
The event is too slow.	Bacterial evolution
The event is too quick.	Pressure changes in an explosion
The location is difficult to reach.	The surface of the moon
Lots of tests would be expensive.	The behaviour of cars in crashes
The event might not happen.	Flooding by a river

Models need **input** such as:
- the temperature of the air
- the rate of bacterial division

Models need **rules** to apply to the data such as:
- how much air expands when heated by a certain amount
- how much nutrient is required by the bacteria

How to make models

Special software can be written to make a model.

Spreadsheets are good tools for modelling. They can use data, formulae and functions to work out what will happen in different circumstances.

The area of the face of a cube and its volume can be modelled in a spreadsheet.

	A	B	C
1	Side length	Area of face	Volume
2	1	1	1
3	2	4	8
4	3	9	27
5	4	16	64
6	5	25	125
7	6	36	216
8			

This is simple to do with a spreadsheet formula.

Computers are useful tools for modelling. You need to understand what models are and why they are important.

20 MINS

	A	B	C
1	Side length	Area of face	Volume
2	1	=A2^2	=A2^3
3	2	=A3^2	=A3^3
4	3	=A4^2	=A4^3
5	4	=A5^2	=A5^3
6	5	=A6^2	=A6^3
7	6	=A7^2	=A7^3
8			

The results can be linked to a chart or graph. It is easy to change the rules and the data.

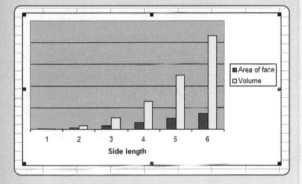

What-if?

Spreadsheets can be used to do 'what-if?' analysis.

- What if we sell twice as many widgets next month? What will our profits be?

- What if twice as many customers visit on Monday? How long will the queues be?

Simulations

Simulations are computer representations of reality. Examples are virtual reality, flight simulators and computer games.

Progress check

1 What is the difference between a computer model and a simulation?

Fill in the gaps.

2 Computer models are useful when predicting the future of house prices. This is because the event is .... The result of this model might well be wrong, because we do not know enough about the .... that affect house prices. We also might not have enough .... about past performances.

3 A computer model is useful when predicting the behaviour of a nuclear power station in meltdown, because the real event is ....

4 A model can be used to predict the movement of the earth's tectonic plates, because the real event is ....

DAY 3

DESKTOP PUBLISHING

What is DTP?

DTP is the process of making and laying out a document by computer. It needs special software such as **Microsoft Publisher** or **Quark Xpress**.

Features of DTP software

Page layout

The way that the columns and different parts of the page are designed can be set up using DTP software. In addition, DTP software has drawing tools to make simple diagrams.

Frames

These are containers of text or graphics on the page. They can be moved about, both on and off the page.

Text flow

Existing text can be flowed into the document. It can be made to flow round graphics.

Templates

A basic page style can be set up and documents are then automatically laid out as required.

Master pages

These contain items that are required on every page.

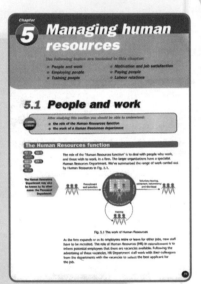

The difference between DTP and word processing

Word processing software can do some things that DTP software can. It can make columns and **import** pictures, but it is not really designed for the job. Professional typesetters need the full range of features that DTP software provides.

Desktop publishing (DTP) is software for laying out publications.

Text

You can type and edit text in a DTP document, but it is best to type text using a word processor and then import it into the DTP document.

DTP software can be used to control the appearance of the text. Not only can you change the font and font size, but also the distance between lines and individual letters.

Graphics

Graphics can come from all sorts of sources:

- digital cameras
- scanned images
- websites
- clip art
- art packages
- drawings

Graphics files come in many **formats**. Some common ones are:

- tagged image format (TIF)
- bitmapped file (BMP)
- joint photographic experts group (JPG or JPEG) – a compressed file type

Progress check

1. How is text prepared for a published page?

2. Give three ways that an image might be prepared for publication in a DTP package.

3. Explain why DTP is better than word processing software for making a newspaper page.

4. State two features present in a DTP package that word processing software does not have.

5. What is a master page?

6. What is a template?

7. What is a frame?

DAY
3

DAY
3

Word processors are for entering and editing text. Text editors can do this as well. Word processors also allow a lot more.

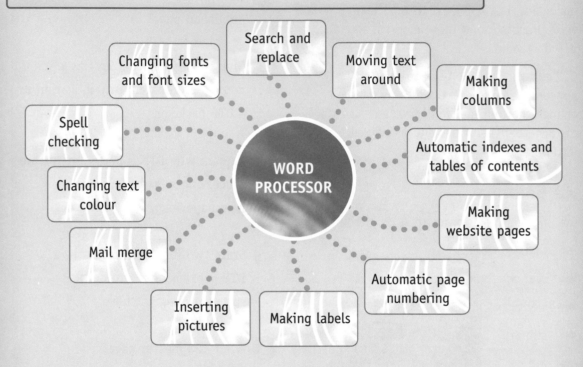

- Search and replace
- Changing fonts and font sizes
- Moving text around
- Making columns
- Spell checking
- Automatic indexes and tables of contents
- Changing text colour
- **WORD PROCESSOR**
- Making website pages
- Mail merge
- Automatic page numbering
- Inserting pictures
- Making labels

● Search and replace

To save a lot of typing, you could write 'OS' instead of 'operating systems', and then replace all occurrences later.

● Spell checkers

These look up words in a dictionary. You need to check their suggestions carefully.

● Images 🖼

Although you can bring images into word processed files, they are difficult to manipulate. DTP is better for this. Also, embedded images make files much larger.

You need to know some of the obvious and not-so-obvious features of word processors.

Mail merge

This involves making lots of similar documents, but with some details changing. The details are merged from a data file.

Cut and paste

It is easy to move text from one place to another, but you have to be careful to tidy up the formatting.

File formats

Word processors can display your work properly because they embed formatting codes in the text. These do not show up, but they:

- add to the file size
- can only be understood properly by the software that created them

Styles

A style is a combination of font, size, colour and spacing. You can apply a style to individual paragraphs or a whole document to make the appearance consistent.

Colour

Word processors can make use of colour. You can highlight text or even change the colour of the screen if is too bright.

Progress check

1. Fill in the gaps.

   Word processors let you move text from one place and put it somewhere else. This is called .... and .... If you wrote a piece about Mr Smith and found later that he was really Mr Smythe, you can use .... and .... to fix all the mistakes at once.

   You can change the font, colour and size of a whole paragraph by using the .... feature.

2. Give three mistakes that a spell checker would not pick up.

3. Give three words that a spell checker could wrongly flag up as incorrect.

4. How could mail merge be used to produce school reports?

5. Explain one way that a word processor can make use of colour to help the user.

DATA LOGGING AND CONTROL

Data logging is when physical data is collected by a hardware device. The data is usually stored for later processing by a computer. Data can be stored on site or transmitted by some form of telemetry (radio or telephone) for processing.

Examples of data logging

- Collecting weather data in a remote location
- Collecting temperature readings in a science experiment
- Collecting temperature data on a remote planet
- Reading distances for a taxi meter
- Reading car speeds for a fuel consumption display
- Reading car number plates for the congestion charge or a speed camera

Sensors

Logging makes use of sensors. These convert physical data into electrical **signals**. Examples are:

- pH
- magnetic
- temperature
- movement
- pressure
- proximity

Sensor signals are usually analogue. You need an analogue/digital converter to pass data to a computer.

Logging period
This is the length of time that the logging goes on. It has to be chosen to cover the whole of the event being logged. It would be a few milliseconds for an explosion, but months for climatic data.

Logging interval
This is the length of time between measurements. It might be every hundredth of a second for measuring tyre temperatures in a Formula 1 car, or every minute in monitoring the pH in a neutralisation reaction.

Advantages of data logging

- No need for a person to be present.
- More accurate than people reading instruments.
- Can work 24/7.
- Can take more readings in a given time.
- Can store the data for computer processing.
- Can work in inhospitable or remote places.

Computers are useful for automating lots of tasks. GCSE exams always ask about this.

Control

This is where the results of data logging are used to control a process. For example:

- the flow of a chemical is measured in a factory and this is used to control the composition of paint

- the temperature of a greenhouse is monitored and used to control the opening of the windows

Advantages of control systems

- Cheaper than using people.

- More accurate than people.

- Control systems don't get tired.

Feedback

This is the passing of signals from a sensor to a computer. A signal is then sent back to an **actuator** to make something happen. If the response of the computer is to reduce something that is increasing or vice versa, this is called **negative feedback**.

Progress check

1. Name three different sensors.

2. What is negative feedback?

3. Suggest a suitable logging period and logging interval for monitoring:
   a) the cooling of a cup of coffee
   b) noise levels near an airport
   c) the rate of flow of a river
   d) the light intensity during a camera flash
   e) the heart rate of a patient

4. What would the sensors and actuators be:
   a) to control traffic lights
   b) to keep a plane at a constant height
   c) to set the shutter speed in an automatic camera?

DAY
3

MISCELLANEOUS SOFTWARE

Computer aided design (CAD)

CAD is used by architects, engineers and designers.

Library of parts: these can be specialised such as a range of kitchen units for a designer.

Scaling: a design can be represented in different sizes.

Line drawings: a full range of tools is available.

FEATURES OF CAD

Calculations: can be used to calculate quantities of materials required for a design.

Flood fill: can be made to simulate different materials such as filling a wall with bricks.

Rotation: designs can be seen from all angles.

Computer aided manufacture (CAM)

This is often associated with CAD. Sometimes designs can be fed as input to machines that make the required article.

Computer aided learning (CAL)

CAL systems help pupils to learn. These vary a great deal from software that provides practice in tests to full-scale systems that track progress through a whole variety of activities.

CAL systems are also much used in schools to demonstrate actions on a set of networked computers in a room.

Computerised axial tomography (CAT)

This is a non-invasive way for doctors to look inside someone's body. An image is built up by computer from signals reflected from internal organs. Tomography means making an image from slices because the body is scanned as a series of imaginary slices.

Expert systems

These are computer systems that are modelled on human experts. They are commonly used for diagnosing problems in machines as well as people. They are more than just a database because they can ask appropriate questions as the result of answers already given.

Expert systems consist of three parts:

- a knowledge base (the facts and rules about the body or machine)

- an inference engine (the software that makes decisions as a result of user inputs)

- an interface (so that it can communicate with the user)

Progress check

1. Fill in the gaps.

   An expert system to find faults in a car contains the facts about the car. This is the ...., the ...., which is the software to analyse answers, and the .... to let it communicate with the technician.

2. State three items that might be stored in the component library of a CAD system used by an architect.

3. State three ways that computers can be used in a school to help pupils learn a subject.

4. What is the connection between CAD and CAM?

5. What is a CAT scan?

6. Why is an expert system about illnesses easier to use than a simple database of symptoms and causes?

DAY 3

BITS AND BYTES

What bytes mean

Computer storage is based on the idea of switches. These can be on or off. On means 1 or true; off means 0 or false. Groups of switches can be used as a code. The code varies according to need.

One switch being on or off is the smallest unit of data. It is called one bit. Usually, data is grouped in packages of at least eight bits that is one byte.

One byte is enough to store:

- a number up to the value 255
- one letter
- part of an instruction in a program

Numbers

These are stored as binary patterns. Just like with ordinary decimal numbers, the value depends on a bit's position. Each position is worth twice that of its neighbour on the right.

Example

value	128	64	32	16	8	4	2	1
bits	0	1	0	0	0	0	0	1

This number is 65 in binary. There is a bit switched on in 64 and 1. Add them up and you get 65.

Letters and other characters

There are codes that match numbers with characters. One common code is ASCII (American Standard Code for Information Interchange). In this code, 65 means capital A. By contrast, unicode can code far more characters than ASCII. It uses 16 bits for each character. It is a way of coding all the characters of all languages.

The bytes can be set to mean **instructions** in a program.

Bytes can represent dots in a **picture** or the loudness, quality and pitch of **music**.

More bytes

A byte is not much data. We need lots of them to be much use. We group them to make bigger units.

Unit	Abbreviation	Equivalent to
Kilobyte	K	2^{10} or 1024 bytes
Megabyte	Mb	2^{10} or 1024 K
Gigabyte	Gb	2^{10} or 1024 Mb

Examples of data quantities

Example	Amount of data
Memory of a typical PC	256 Mb
Storage capacity of a floppy disk	1.44 Mb
Storage capacity of a typical hard disk	40 Gb
Storage capacity of a typical CD	600 Mb
A picture that fills the screen	Between 1 and 2 Mb

Other uses for bits

Bits can be used to switch things on and off. In a machine, a bit can switch a motor on when it is 1 and off when it is 0. Complex machines can be controlled by lots of bits.

Progress check

1. Give three ways that a bit pattern can be interpreted by a computer.

2. Name a code that is used to store letters or characters.

3. How many bytes are there in 2 Mb?

4. Why do documents with embedded pictures often not fit onto floppy disks?

5. What is the smallest quantity of data that can be stored?

DAY
4

DATA TYPES AND DATABASES

All data is stored in the same way – as a binary bit pattern. A computer can be set to interpret bit patterns in lots of different ways.

Data type	Meaning	Amount of storage needed
Text (also called string)	Any group of characters including numbers, letters, spaces and symbols	1 byte per character
Integers (numbers with no fractions or decimal places)	Pure numbers only No characters or decimal points allowed	Usually between 1 and 4 bytes, but can be more
Real or fractional numbers	Decimal points allowed	Typically between 4 and 12 bytes – depends on precision required
Dates	Can include dates and times in many systems	Typically 8 bytes
Alphabetic	Letters only	1 byte per character
Alphanumeric	Letters and numbers only	1 byte per character
Boolean (Yes/No)	True or false only	1 bit
Currency	Money values only	8 bytes
Memo	Long text entries	1 byte per character

Examples

Example fields	Data type	Reason
Telephone number	Text or alphanumeric	Need to include spaces and leading zeroes
Postcode	Text or alphanumeric	Contains letters and numbers
Income	Currency	Displays with two decimal places and calculations are accurate
Date borrowed (in a library)	Date/time	Allows calculations so that date due back can be worked out
Surname	Text or alphabetic	Made of letters only

Databases

Databases are organised stores of data. The data is grouped in a regular way.

Databases are not software. They are created and handled by database software.

Flat file databases

Flat file databases are simple databases made of **fields** and **records**. There are no links between different data stores. They are like a card index and suitable for things like simple address books.

Relational databases

- Relational databases are made from a collection of **tables**.

- The tables are **linked** together, by **key fields**. Each record is identified by a unique primary key. The primary keys can also appear as links in other tables where they are foreign keys.

- Data is independent of the software that created it.

- Each data item (except linking fields) is stored once only to make sure that only the one up-to-date item is used. This is called **non-redundancy**.

Progress check

1 What data type only takes one bit of storage?

2 What data type is suitable for storing a telephone number?

3 What is the basic storage container in a relational database?

4 What is a simple database with just one set of records called?

5 Why do relational databases store each item of data just once?

Files

A file is a store of data on a computer system. It usually has a name such as holiday.mdb. A file may contain many different parts.

Files come in various types: structured and illustrated.

In databases, the data is organised. The employees of a company all have the same data stored about them – their names, addresses and pay rates. This data is **structured**. Structured data is easier to process than unstructured. Sometimes unstructured files are used:

- pictures
- sounds
- programs

Tables

In **relational** databases the data is stored in **tables**. A table is set up for each **entity**. An entity is a thing about which data is stored such as a person or a car or an invoice.

The things that we need to know are called **fields**. A field is one item of information about an entity. For example, for a pupil, fields will include the name and date of birth.

All the fields for one individual or entity make up one **record**.

Key fields

In most tables, one of the fields is set up as a **key field**. This is a special field that identifies the record. It is usually a reference number to make sure that it is unique.

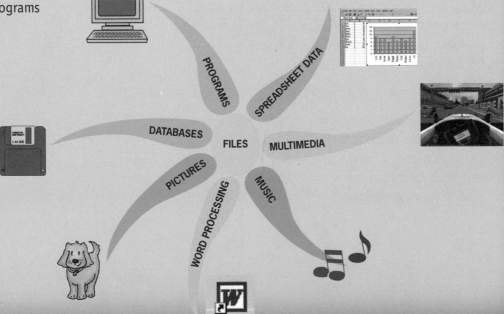

DAY 4

1 2 3 4 5 6 7

Databases usually store data in well-organised structures. This makes it a lot easier to process.

20 MINS

Record types

Records may be a fixed length or a variable length.

Fixed length fields

The size of each record is determined in advance.

> Advantages of fixed length files:
>
> - you know how much space they will take up.
> - it is easy to find a record, because they are all the same size

Fixed length files waste space. If a field is set up as 20 bytes and the data is 4 bytes, 16 bytes are wasted.

Variable length fields

The record size is not determined in advance. Each field is separated from the next by a marker such as a comma.

> Advantages of variable length files:
>
> - they grow as required and so there is no need to determine the size in advance
> - they don't waste space

Variable length fields are often separated by commas. Files like these can be read by many types of software, and are called **comma separated variable (CSV)** files.

Progress check

1. What data structure holds the data about one entity?

2. What is the data about one individual called?

3. What is a field?

4. Give one advantage of using fixed length fields.

5. Give one advantage of using variable length fields.

6. What is a CSV file?

7. What is a key field?

8. What would be a suitable key field for a table of car data?

9. What is an entity?

10. What is a file?

ACCURACY: VALIDATION AND VERIFICATION

Accuracy

You can never be absolutely sure that data entered is accurate, but there are lots of ways to make it as likely as possible.

Reduce typing

It is less likely that mistakes will be made if data is selected from alternatives instead of being typed in. For example:

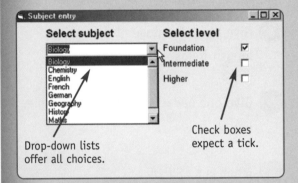

Drop-down lists offer all choices.

Check boxes expect a tick.

Codes

The less typing involved, the fewer mistakes. You are more likely to hit a wrong key if you enter 'paid by credit card' than if you enter the code 'C'.

Validation

Validation is the **checking** of data by the **computer** when it is **input** to make sure that it is **sensible/acceptable**.
It is not checking that data is **correct**.

Types of validation

There are lots of ways that data can be validated. Here are some examples.

- **Length check** – the data must not be too long or too short.
- **Type check** – the data must be the right type such as number.
- **Presence check** – some fields must be filled in.
- **Format check** – the data must fit a pattern, such as a postcode.
- **Check digit** – a calculation produces an extra digit. When entered again, the same calculation must produce the same result.
- **Range check** – the data must be between certain values.

Get Away Travel

Bookings screen

If an entry is wrong, an error message will appear.

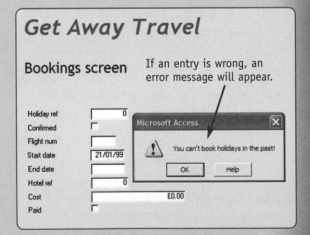

It is vital that data entered into a computer is reliable. Bad data can cost money, be inconvenient or even life-threatening. The computer can be set to reject data that doesn't make sense.

Verification

Verification is the checking of data, often by a person or a person with help from a computer, to ensure that data is **correct**.

Double entry verification

- Two people enter the data separately (they are unlikely to make the same mistakes).

- The computer then compares the two versions.

- The computer flags up the differences.

- The source document is checked.

This makes twice the work, but sometimes it is worth it.

Parity check

- A computer checks that data is correct.

- Used when transmitting data between devices.

- With **even parity** the number of 1s in each byte must be even (e.g. 00101101 has four 1s). Some systems use odd parity instead.

- One bit is the parity bit. If a byte has an odd number of 1s, the parity bit is flipped to 1 to fix this. Otherwise, it is left as 0.

- Any byte with an odd number must be wrong, so retransmission is requested.

Progress check

1. When does validation take place?

2. Someone types in 'Mr Jones' instead of 'Mr Johns'. How can an error like this be detected?

3. Someone types in 'Mr J9nes' instead of 'Mr Jones'. How can this error be detected?

4. What is a parity bit?

5. In a system using even parity, which of these bytes has been transmitted incorrectly?
   a) 01100110
   b) 00111001
   c) 00111011

6. An exam board lets examiners enter student marks online. The examiners have to enter the marks twice. Why is this? What is this process called?

7. This is a valid UK car registration number: VX04ABC. What validation checks can be used to reduce errors on input?

DAY 4

DATA INPUT AND OUTPUT

Data capture

Out there in the world is lots of information. If we want to process it in a database, first we have to capture it. It then becomes data.

You can capture data in lots of ways. Automatic methods such as barcodes, optical mark recognition (OMR) and optical character recognition (OCR) are the most likely to be consistent and accurate.

Sometimes we have to make forms for people to fill in. These are called **data capture forms**. They are sometimes called questionnaires. Data capture forms must be easy and quick to fill in, otherwise people won't bother.

Advantages of data capture forms:

- everyone gets asked the same questions
- everyone will answer the questions in much the same way
- people might be more honest than in a face-to-face interview
- lots of forms can be sent out
- the data can be processed easily because it is all in the same format

Rules for data capture forms

Data capture forms must:

- be clear
- be easy to fill in
- have a title so that you know what it's about
- have all the information you need
- have a useful prompt for each question
- have instructions on how to enter things, e.g. date of birth (dd/mm/yy)
- have tick boxes wherever possible
- have boxes for entering letters

Disadvantages of questionnaires:

- often people cannot be bothered with them
- sometimes people want to give different sorts of answers that aren't possible on the form

Computers exist to produce output. However, first of all we need something to input.

Screen forms

Some data capture forms are on computer screens instead of paper. The same rules apply as for paper forms except that screen forms:

- don't have a box for each letter

- have check boxes, radio buttons and pull-down boxes (combo boxes)

- have buttons to confirm or cancel

Output from a database

We rarely want to see everything in a database. The whole point in using them is so that we can quickly extract a **subset** of what is there.

Screen output is for enquiries when we do not need to keep the results.

Paper output from a database is called a **report**. Reports can:

- sort data in any order

- group data by category

Paper output is also called **hard copy**.

Data capture!

DAY 4

⊙ Searching

A relational database is made up of tables. There may be lots of them. We often want to find a particular combination of data that may come from more than one table.

Database software lets us find what we need quickly. Most database software is flexible so that we can ask new questions.

Example

A bank might want to ask 'What are the names and addresses of all the customers who are overdrawn?' For this, the software would have to look in the customer table and the accounts tables at the very least.

⊙ Types of search

A user can search for data in many different ways.

Method	Example
By entering a key word	A customer name
By selecting a search task that has already been set up	To display all outstanding invoices
By working through menus of choices	Customers → Accounts → Maintenance → New customers

⊙ How the software finds data

Finding data in a relational database makes use of **queries**.
Queries need to know several things.

- What data are you looking for? (The fields)

- Where is it? (The table(s) where the data is stored)

- What are the conditions (criteria) for the search (such as date is today AND status is overdrawn)?

Databases are often extremely large. We use software to find what we want in them.

15 MINS

AND and OR

- To match more than one condition, use the word **AND**.
- If we want to match alternative conditions, we use the word **OR**.

A query can be expressed in words.

Example

```
SELECT customer_name,
customer_address
FROM customer_table
WHERE date=today
AND status="O/D"
```

Conditions

A search can look for things in different ways.

Search condition	Example
Match	NAME="Smith"
Those that are bigger than some value	AGE>21
Those that are smaller than some value	SALARY<25000
Those that are between two values	WEIGHT>4 AND WEIGHT<10

Indexes

Finding data in a big database can take a long time. Indexes are extra files that speed up searches. Indexes tell the software where to look for a particular item, just like a book index tells you which page to go to.

Progress check

1. What word can be used in a query to link two conditions?

2. How could you set up a query to find all the customers between the ages of 20 and 30?

3. What can be added to a database to make searches quicker?

4. What three things does database software need to know to find particular records in a relational database?

5. What does this query mean in plain English?

   SELECT make, colour
   FROM cars
   WHERE make="Peugeot"
   AND colour="Red"

File types

Files can be classified according to their purpose.

Type	Description	Example
Master files	Contain the most important data that the company owns. Do not change often. Usually stored in key field order.	Supermarket's stock file
Transaction files	Contain a record of things that have happened over a period. Change all the time. Stored in chronological order.	Today's sales
Archives	Contain old data that may be needed in the future.	Last year's sales figures
Backups	Extra copies of files kept in case of data loss.	All the company data

Updating files

Real-time

Some files are updated immediately the data changes. Bookings such as flights, hotel rooms or concerts need to be updated in real-time (as they happen) so that double bookings do not occur.

Batch

Master files are updated by being merged with the transaction file. For example, the amount of an item in stock can be adjusted at the end of the day by taking away the number that are recorded as sold in the transaction file. The transaction file must be **sorted** before this can be done.

Generations

When a master file is updated, a new master file is produced. The new file is called the **son** file. The old master file is called the **father** file. The **father** file from the previous update is called the **grandfather** file.

There are some common operations that are performed on files.

Usually the grandfather file is recycled at the next update and becomes the new son file again.

Progress check

1. What sort of file stores the books borrowed from the library in one day?

2. What sort of file stores details of all the books in the library?

3. In what order are the records in a transaction file?

4. In what order are the records in a master file?

5. What is a son file?

FILE ACCESS METHODS

The user of a database or any other stored data does not need to know how the data is actually stored. Only the software needs to know so that it can retrieve what is wanted as efficiently as possible. Software designers use different methods according to the nature of the data.

Database files

Data in databases is usually **structured**. It is stored in a regular, repeating pattern. It is often stored as a set of records which may be in a database table or in a file that is stored separately. Each record is made up of fields.

Serial files

In serial files the records are stored one after another. There is no particular order except possibly chronological. Transaction files are often stored in serial files. To add a new record, the software locates the end of the file and writes the record. To find a record, start at the beginning and look at each record until found or the end of the file is reached. Serial files are slow to find records. They can be stored on disk or tape.

Sequential files

To remember sequential files, think of a sequence like 1, 2, 3.

In sequential files the records are stored one after another. The records are in some order, usually key field. Master files are sometimes stored in sequential files.
To add a new record:

> copy the records of the old file onto a new file until you reach the place where the new record should go

> write the new record to the new file at that point

> copy the rest of the old file to the new file

To find a record, start at the beginning and look at each record until found, or stop when a record with greater key value is found, then stop. It can be quicker to find records in sequential files than in an unsorted serial file. They also can be stored on disk or tape.

Indexed sequential files

These are like sequential files except the position of a block of data can be looked up in the index. The software can fast forward to that point and then start looking. This means it is much faster when the files are large.

Random (direct) access files

Random access file records are stored on disk (not tape). The position on the disk is determined by a calculation done on the key field. Records can be retrieved directly with less need to search through earlier records. Access is fast and so they are suitable for bookings and other real-time applications.

⬭ Other data stores

Not all data is structured (e.g. pictures, music, video, programs, documents). These are known as binary files. In these cases, the data is read in a byte at a time until the end of the file is reached.

Progress check

1. What file type stores records in no particular order?

2. What file type is suitable for storing airline timetables?

3. How can access to a sequential file be speeded up?

4. What is a binary file?

5. What storage medium is necessary for random (direct) access files?

6. What type of file storage is suitable for a file of employees in a company?

DAY 4

DAY 5

IT projects

Think of IT projects as real-life work rather than something you have to do as part of your coursework. This will give it much more sense.

IT projects are usually commissioned by someone (the client) from a software developer. The client pays, so is the most important person in a project. The developer is usually a company, not an individual.

In real life, IT projects often:

- are complex and expensive
- involve inventing things that have not existed before
- involve lots of people with a wide variety of skills
- need good communication between team members and with the client

Methods have been developed to try to keep IT projects under control so that they are completed in time and within budget

IT projects follow fairly well-defined stages. These stages help to make sure that nothing is left out. They also make it easier for different project members to understand each other.

You need to know what goes on at each stage of system development.

System development is sometimes called the **system lifecycle**, because development never really comes to an end.

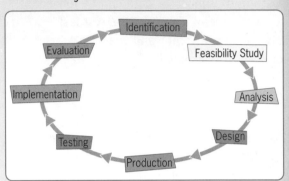

Identifying the problem

What types of problems are suitable for computers to solve?

- **Lots of repetition:** Computers are good at doing the same thing over and over. They don't get bored.

- **Great need for accuracy:** Computers don't make mistakes. If they are set up correctly, they are exceptionally reliable.

- **Human solution too expensive:** In the long run, computer solutions can be cheaper than employing people.

- **Lots of data:** It can take a long time to process many transactions.

- **Speed is essential:** Sometimes it is important to see results straight away, such as enquiring about a bank balance or adjusting the flaps on an aircraft.

Finding out what is needed

If a client wants a computer solution, the **analyst** needs to find out exactly what the problem is. The client might only have a rough idea. The usual methods are as follows.

- **Interview:** this allows for follow-up questions.

- **Questionnaires:** lots of people can be asked the same questions, but they might not all reply.

- **Observation:** watching people work can reveal efficiency issues.

- **Paperwork:** the existing methods might be inefficient and so looking at the paperwork helps understanding.

Requirements specification

After discussions with the client, the analysts will produce a requirements specification. This is a list of the things that the system must do.

Progress check

1. Who is the most important person in an IT project?

2. What person investigates the needs of a project?

3. State two ways of investigating a problem.

4. Give two characteristics of a problem that make it suitable for a computer solution.

5. Give two reasons why it is good to have a standard method for solving problems.

6. State two of the common stages of the system lifecycle.

DAY 5

Breaking down the problem

Once a problem has been identified and a list of requirements drawn up, it needs to be broken down into its parts. Breaking it down helps to focus on simpler tasks and lets you allocate parts of the project to different people.

The main sections to look at are:

Output – what the system must produce (this is what the client is interested in)

Input – what must go into the system to allow for the right output

Processing – the actions necessary to get the output

Stage	What needs to be considered	How it can be documented
Output	Screen, paper, sounds, actions	Preliminary drawings, diagrams, descriptions
Input	Screen, sound, signals from devices	Preliminary drawings, descriptions
Processing	Program modules, spreadsheet formulae, database queries	Plans, flow charts

The analysis looks at the main stages and documents are drawn up that provide an overview of the proposed system.

Diagrams and flow charts

Data flow diagrams show entities (often these are people), processes, data stores and the flow of data between them.

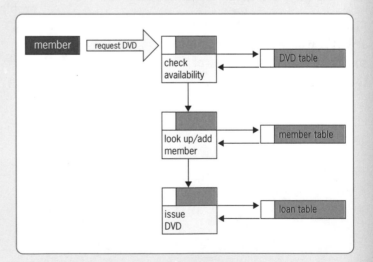

System flow charts show the details of data stores, processes and input and output.

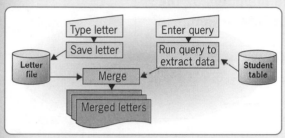

Process boxes should have verbs in them, while data stores and output documents should have nouns in them.

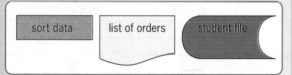

● Prototypes

This is a mock-up of the proposed solution. The client can then accept this or suggest changes.

● Security

Keeping data safe is an important part of the planning.

- **Reliability:** validation checks will be built in to reduce mistakes in data input.
- **Integrity:** a backup strategy makes sure that there is always a good copy of data in case data is **corrupted**.
- **Safety:** measures will be taken to protect data against unauthorised access and destruction.

Progress check

1. Draw a system flow chart shape suitable to hold a file of stock in a shop.

2. What type of word goes into a process box?

3. What is a prototype used for?

4. What is data corruption?

5. Give one way that data can be protected from corruption.

6. How can a system be set up to reduce data input errors?

7. Give two reasons why big projects are broken down before being solved.

An IT project consists of many parts. They all need to be designed. The designs are usually given to members of the project team, notably programmers, to put into action.

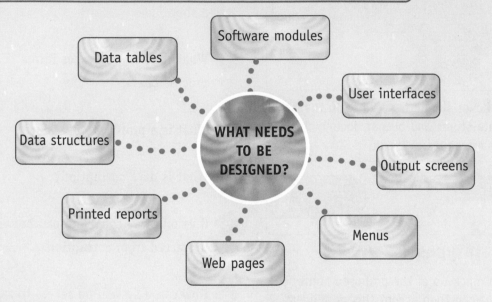

Data tables

Software modules

User interfaces

Data structures

WHAT NEEDS TO BE DESIGNED?

Output screens

Printed reports

Menus

Web pages

Data tables

Most databases are relational. Each table will hold data about a single entity, such as a customer or a car.

- The data type of each field is decided.

- The size of each field is specified.

- Validation rules are decided.

- Key fields decided on.

- Indexes are chosen that will speed data access.

- Input formats are specified such as the proper layout of postcodes.

Data structures

Most IT projects involve databases. Databases need to be structured so that they can be processed accurately. Decisions must be made about whether a database is to be relational.

Software modules

Programs are written in 'chunks' or modules. The design team lays down what must happen in each module and hands these designs to the programmers.

Once the basic parts of a system have been determined, these parts need to be designed in detail so that they can be implemented by others.

20 MINS

Some processing is not written from scratch.

Example

In database management systems, queries can be produced without having to write any program code. However, the parts of the system must be designed to work together.

User interfaces

Each screen must be designed so that it is easy to use. Well-designed user-friendly interfaces reduce mistakes and ensure people like working with them. The user interface includes input and output screens and how the menus link the parts together.

Printed reports

Most software produces printed output. These should be carefully designed so that they fulfil the needs of the client.

Websites

Site maps need to be made so that the people who make the website know how to link the pages together.

● The client

Designs should be shown to the client in case any changes are needed before the system is built.

Progress check

1. Why are designs necessary for IT projects?

2. What features make a good user interface?

3. What should designers do before they hand their designs to the rest of the project team?

4. State three decisions that have to be made when designing a data table.

5. What is a database index for?

6. What is the printed output from a database called?

DAY 5

1
2
3
4
6
7

Implementation

- Implementation is making the product. It is also about installing it and handing it over to the client.

- The data structures are created. Often this is done with special software tools. The details of the data structures are stored in a **data dictionary** which is a database about the database.

- The reports are created. This can be done with special report-building software.

- The program code is written. Often the different modules are written by different programmers. This makes use of their special skills and gets the project finished more quickly.

- The screens are created. These can be made by dragging objects from a toolbox onto a form, so reducing the amount of programming.

Training

To get the best out of a new system, the staff should be trained. This can cost a lot, but it is worth it in the long run. There is no point in having a good computer system if it is not used to the fullest possible extent.

Testing

Computer systems must be tested before being handed over to the client. Testing means deliberately trying to show faults in the system. A good test is one that uncovers a fault.

Testing must be planned. Test data is invented to cover situations that are expected in use and also to anticipate unusual occurrences. For each test, the tester should record:

- test number

- the part of the system being tested

- test data

- expected result

- actual result

- action taken

Alpha testing is carried out by the software developers.

Beta testing is carried out by specially-chosen users who report faults back to the developers.

Roll out

When the system has been thoroughly tested, it is installed at the client's premises. There are different strategies for doing this.

Direct changeover: The new system takes over straight away.

> **Advantage** – The user has the benefits of the new system as soon as possible. It can be cheaper to abandon the old system straight away.
>
> **Disadvantage** – If there are any problems, the client cannot revert to the old system.

Parallel run: The new system runs alongside the old one.

> **Advantage** – If there are problems, the old system is still working as a backup.
>
> **Disadvantage** – Work has to be done twice and this increases costs.

Pilot run: Only part of the system is implemented until it is clear that it works well.

> **Advantage** – If there are problems, only part of the organisation is affected.
>
> **Disadvantage** – It takes longer for the benefits to be applied to the whole organisation.

Progress check

1. What is a pilot run?

2. What makes a good test?

3. Give three things that testers should record for each test.

4. What is a data dictionary?

5. Why are the program modules of a project often written by different programmers?

6. What is the difference between alpha and beta testing?

SYSTEM DOCUMENTATION

Why is documentation so important?

Software is usually quite complex. Documentation is meant to reduce the likelihood of errors and help in communications.

Documentation can be time-consuming and expensive to produce, but it is worth it to help to solve problems later.

Technical documentation

This is aimed at computer professionals.

- Programmers
- Installers
- System managers

Documentation for programmers

Computer systems can be updated by programmers who did not work on the original. Good documentation helps new programmers to understand how the software was put together.

If there are problems later, the documentation also serves as evidence that everything was done properly.

Documentation for installers

Those who set the system up – system administrators, managers and installers – do not need to know about the program code, just how to install the system.

The installers should make their own notes too. If they hit a problem during installation, they can then go back to where the problem occurred.

Documentation for programmers	Documentation for installers
Data flow	The system requirements
Data structure details	File locations
Program source code	The network layout for which it is intended
Explanations of how modules communicate	How to fix errors
Test data and test	Security features results

Every stage of producing a system should be documented. Different types of documentation are aimed at different types of people.

20
MINS

User documentation

The end user needs documentation so as to make the best of the system. User documentation should include:

- how to start the system

- how to make use of all its features such as entering new data, saving data and printing reports

- what error messages mean

- what to do when errors occur

- the answers to frequently asked questions (FAQs)

- a step-by-step tutorial that can take the user through an example situation

Types of documentation

Documentation can be provided:

- a paper manual can be read anywhere, but can get lost and out of date

- documentation on a CD needs to be read at a computer, but it can be copied and is easily replaced by newer versions

- documentation on a website can be kept completely up to date and it can take useful information from the user to help with marketing or planning future products

Progress checks

1. State two sections that should be in:
   a) programmer documentation
   b) installation documentation
   c) user documentation

2. Give an advantage of supplying documentation:
   a) on a CD
   b) on a website
   c) as a book

3. Why is it important for a system installer to keep notes?

4. State two problems that may occur if a user does not bother to read the documentation.

5. What is a software tutorial?

DAY
5

Evaluation

Evaluation is not the same as testing. Evaluation is assessing the success or otherwise of the system. It is done mostly by the end user or client.

Success criteria

Does the system meet the requirements specification?

If the system does not do what the customer originally wanted, there might be a case for delaying payment. In some cases, court action may follow.

Does the system perform well?

There may be performance issues. Perhaps the system is slow or does not work well when other programs are running.

Is the system easy to use?

The system might work properly, but the users don't like it. They can be asked about it or can be given questionnaires to complete.

Are there any compatibility problems?

It could be that the system is not compatible with the old data and a lot of data has to be re-entered.

New features

When a system is evaluated, it is common for people to have ideas about what would be good to add to it. Possibly some new reports would help or a wider variety of ways to search for data. Evaluation can often include ideas that can be implemented when the software is next updated.

Maintenance

Users' needs change and computers' systems need to change with them. Maintenance is changing a system after it has been delivered. There can be various reasons for making changes to a system.

Corrective changes

There may be errors that were not discovered during testing. The user might have to pay for these to be fixed if this was not included in the original contract. Sometimes, extra modules of program code called **patches** can be added to the system to fix a problem.

Perfective changes

The users might see ways of doing jobs better. The developers might be called back to make improvements to the user interface of the layout of the modules or reports.

Adaptive changes

The client may have new needs such as a new operating system, there may be new aspects to the client's business or new laws that have been changed which affect the way of working.

Maintenance can be expensive. Some systems are 50 years old or more and are still being maintained.

Progress check

1. What are performance criteria?

2. Who is the most important person to involve when evaluating a system?

3. What is perfective maintenance and why might it be carried out?

4. State two problems that might occur with a new piece of software.

5. Apart from the start-up costs, list three other things that a company must budget for when changing to a new system.

What is the Internet?

The Internet connects computers together across the world, using telecommunication links.

Connecting to the Internet

To connect, you need:

- a computer
- an ISP (Internet service provider)
- a router or a modem

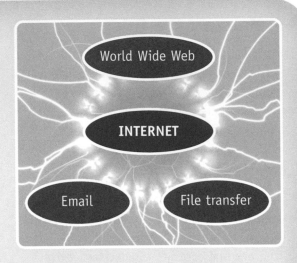

World Wide Web

INTERNET

Email

File transfer

Protocols

Protocols are rules that govern how data is transmitted. There are rules for the different types of communication, but most come under the heading of **TCP/IP (transmission control protocol/Internet protocol)**.

HTTP stands for hypertext transfer protocol: the set of rules for transmitting web pages. Hypertext is text that contains **hyperlinks** – the words or images that can be clicked on to take the user to another page or part of a page.

FTP stands for file transfer protocol: the rules for transmitting data files over the Internet. FTP is used for downloading music or publications as well as for sending web pages to a service provider.

Making and viewing web pages

Web pages are text files. They can be written with a simple text editor, although most people use authoring software. Web pages are constructed with **HTML (hypertext markup language)**. This is a system of tags and other instructions that determine how a web page will look when viewed in a browser.

A **browser** is software that interprets and displays web pages.

URL stands for uniform resource locator. This is the address of a website or other resource.

Domain name system: This is the way that an Internet resource is located. Each website or other resource has a unique domain name. This is looked up on a **domain name server**, which translates it into an **IP address**. An IP address is a set of four numbers that uniquely identifies a device on the Internet.

In the URL:

http://letts-education.com

letts-education.com is the domain name.

Services provided on the Internet

- **Chat:** Some websites allow real-time interactive conversations or chat rooms.

- **Search engine:** This program searches a database of websites in response to a user's enquiry.

Bandwidth

Bandwidth refers to the number of signals that can be sent along a medium at the same time. It affects transmission speeds. Fast digital connections are called **broadband**. Broadband is necessary for transmitting big files for:

- films
- music
- video conferencing

Compression

Images, music and other large files are often compressed before transmission to make them download faster. JPEG, GIF and MPEG are common compression standards.

Progress check

1. What is a protocol?

2. Name two protocols associated with the Internet.

3. What is a domain name?

4. Fill in the gaps.

   The Internet is a way of connecting millions of .... by using .... links. The three major services that are provided by the Internet are ...., ... and ....

5. Why are image files often compressed before being sent over the Internet, but word processed documents are usually not?

Billions of emails are sent each day. They are fast becoming one of the most important ways that businesses and private individuals communicate. People call old-fashioned mail 'snail mail', because it is usually slower.

Advantages and disadvantages of email

ADVANTAGES	DISADVANTAGES
• It is usually delivered much faster than ordinary mail.	• It is easy to be misunderstood. (The absence of tone of voice can cause problems.)
• It is cheaper to send.	• It is tempting to be hasty and, often, emails can be regretted.
• Time zones do not matter, so it can be more convenient than telephoning someone.	• It is not secure, others can intercept it.
• Emails can be copied to lots of people in one go.	• It is abused by spammers.
• It is quick and easy to reply.	
• Any computer file can be sent as an attachment.	

Spam

Spam is unwanted advertising emails sent out in bulk. Spam wastes time and bandwidth. Some spam can be blocked by filters, but spammers keep finding new ways to get through. Spam sometimes contains viruses, so it is important to be careful about opening attachments. Replying to spam confirms that it has reached an active address. Often, emails that are from someone you don't know are spam.

DAY 6

Email questions are common in exams. If you have sent emails, you should be able to answer these questions.

Features of email software

Email software provides:

- a space for the message
- a 'To' box
- a subject box so that the recipient can quickly see what a message is about
- a CC (carbon copy) box for anyone else you want to send the message to
- a BCC (blind carbon copy) box, when you don't want all the other addresses where you are sending the message to show
- address books with email addresses of your contacts

Types of email software

There are two main types of email software:

- web-based
- client-based

Web-based email:

- can be accessed anywhere
- may have storage restrictions
- may contain adverts
- may be more prone to spam

Client-based email software is used by most businesses and it can be set up to be accessed remotely.

Progress check

1 a) Give two advantages of email over ordinary mail.

b) Give two advantages of email over the telephone.

2 Give two reasons why spam costs legitimate Internet users money.

3 Give one advantage and one disadvantage of using web-based email services.

4 What are these features of email software?
a) CC
b) BCC

5 Why should you not reply to spam?

DATA SECURITY

The importance of data

Businesses depend on their data. The data helps them to run their activities and to plan for the future. Most data is stored on computer systems.

Dangers to data

It can be lost

- A hard disk crashes.
- A computer is stolen.
- Someone accidentally deletes data.

It can be damaged

- A disk can have a fault.
- A virus can damage data.
- A disgruntled employee can interfere with data.

It can be illegally accessed or stolen

- Private details can be seen by hackers.
- Business rivals can steal plans.

Viruses and worms

A **virus** is a program that replicates itself. It often causes damage. It may attach itself to other programs. A **worm** is a virus that stands alone from other programs.

Trojan horses and spyware

Trojan horses are programs that enter a computer disguised as something else. Some are spyware which are to report user activities back to their originator across the Internet.

Users can reduce the danger of malicious software by:

- using up-to-date virus scanners
- using anti-spyware software
- installing a firewall
- not opening suspicious emails
- not using pirated software

Hacking

This is the unauthorised access of computer files. Often it is achieved by guessing passwords. Hackers sometimes just copy data, or they may alter it.

Integrity

This is the state of data remaining in its original condition. It can be changed by hackers, viruses or system faults.

Reliability

Data must be correct if it is to be of any use. Validation and verification help to safeguard reliability.

Data is vitally important to all organisations. It must to be protected against loss or damage. Exam questions often ask about how this is done.

Passwords

Networks, files and database tables can be protected by passwords. Passwords should be changed regularly and not be obvious.

Encryption

Data can be transformed so that it is indecipherable if intercepted. The recipient needs a private 'key' to decrypt it.

Physical security

Valuable data can be stored on stand-alone computers or in locked rooms.

Biometrics

Access to computers can be controlled by fingerprint or retina scans.

Firewalls

These are combinations of hardware and software that control access to a network or computer from outside. They can also control access to resources from the computer or network itself.

Backups

These are the key to most security issues. Backups can be fallen back on in case of disaster. They can be made on CD, tape or memory sticks and stored elsewhere, possibly online.

Backups might be incremental, where only updated files are backed up.

Please enter your password.

Later ...

Someone's guessed my password.

Teletext

Teletext is an old system of transmitting information via part of a TV signal. It can be accessed on most TVs. It is mostly still transmitted in analogue signals. It is slow to access, does not provide proper graphics and is not interactive.

Interactive television

Modern digital TV systems allow users to send data back to the TV provider as well as to receive information. The large bandwidth available in the digital channels used allows much more than just TV signals to be transmitted. Telephone or cable connections can be used to send signals back to the providers.

By using the handset, viewers can:

- vote in surveys
- change views in sporting events
- order a film.

It is also possible to access email, but that is easier if a proper keyboard is attached.

Telephone services

Most businesses have a private internal telephone exchange. This uses IT to:

- direct callers to the right person
- maintain queues of callers
- play messages or music to callers on hold
- respond to key presses to divert callers to different departments
- make automatic calls to customers
- send automatic text messages

The IT system can also monitor calls, display how long people are waiting to be answered and how many are in the queue. It can be very annoying to wait in a telephone queue, especially when you have to pay for the call by the second.

Call centres

This can be located anywhere in the world. Operators have databases of customers or contacts and distance makes no difference. Many call centres are being set up in India to handle business in the UK.

Call centres make use of technology:

- to telephone people for advertising purposes

- to process orders for goods and services

- to manage bank accounts

It is possible that the examiner who marks your GCSE exam paper will telephone the marks to the examining body through a call centre.

Mobile telephones

There are ever-increasing numbers of services available from mobile phones:

- internet access

- text messaging, known as short message service (SMS)

- taking and sending photos

- travel enquiries

- share dealing

Press 1 to place an order.

Press 2 to pay a bill.

Press 3 to jump to the front of the queue.

ECOMMERCE

The Internet started as a way for universities to communicate. It has now become a significant medium for doing business. Ecommerce covers the many ways that business can be conducted over the Internet.

Business to business (B2B)

Businesses have communicated by computer for a long time, but the growth of the Internet has made this easier. So, more and more businesses place their orders online. This has advantages:

- speed
- accuracy
- easier record keeping

Much more business is done by email. Multinational companies can send files between offices rapidly and without having to worry about time zones.

However, people spend a large part of their working day sorting out their messages and deleting spam.

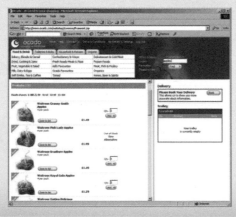

New markets

Existing businesses have found that the Internet allows them to expand their activities. Through their websites they can:

- reach a global audience
- offer new services
- respond quickly to market trends
- reduce the size of their premises
- relocate to cheaper areas

Ecommerce is more than just advertising. As websites can be interactive, customers can place orders online.

Websites need to be set up in different languages and to take account of local sensitivities.

New ways of doing old business

Most supermarkets sell goods online so that busy or disabled people can buy groceries without having to go to the shop.

The Internet has provided a whole new way of doing business. You should be able to quote many different examples.

Advantages to the consumer

Ecommerce can increase trade. Businesses can hold big stocks with a wide variety of products and locate them in cheaper areas.

Customers can shop around without having to leave home. They can get the best deals more easily than before. Many goods can be bought cheaper by shopping in a different country and there is more choice.

Customers can track the progress of their orders and accounting is more accurate.

New businesses

The Internet has made it possible to do business in lots of new ways. Examples of successful business ventures that do not involve goods are:

- travel services
- insurance
- banking
- share dealing

There was a time when lots of new businesses started up at the same time to take advantage of online business opportunities. These were called **dotcoms** after their web addresses. Many failed because there was not enough of a market for all.

Progress check

1. State three activities that businesses might use the Internet for when dealing with other companies.

2. State three advantages to the consumer of doing business online.

3. Who might want to make use of online grocery shopping?

4. Give two advantages of buying books online.

5. How can ebusiness help to bring prices down?

6. How can ebusiness help a business to expand?

DAY 6

Accounting

Most businesses use IT methods to do calculations. This allows them to trade more efficiently and to make fewer mistakes when dealing with business partners and customers.

EPOS (electronic point of sale)

All supermarkets check out goods at EPOS terminals. These scan the barcodes on goods and look up the prices in a database, then add up and print an itemised bill. This makes customers happy because:

- they are served more quickly

- fewer mistakes are made in their bills

- they can check the prices of what they bought later

This helps the shop because:

- it can serve more customers in the same time

- it needs fewer staff

- it keeps useful records such as which till operators are working the fastest

EFTPOS (electronic funds transfer at point of sale)

This is an extension of EPOS. It lets the customer pay for the goods without cash. The customer uses a credit or debit card. This is good for customers and shops because:

- the shop receives the money immediately

- there is less of a security problem when shops hold less cash

- the customer can ask for 'cash back' from a debit card

- detailed records can be kept

Loyalty cards

Customers can join a loyalty card scheme and are awarded points according to how much they spend. These can be used for a variety of purposes such as money off or special offers. They are useful to the shops because they can use computer systems to find out who is buying what. This is useful in planning and marketing. Some loyalty cards are shared by a number of businesses.

Loyalty cards can also be used for promotions by offering extra points. Some shops send money-off coupons to their members and these can be tailored to fit the shopping habits of each customer.

DAY 7

One way that ICT has greatly affected our lives is in the way we shop and you need to be aware of some of the details.

Stock control and ordering

EPOS can be linked to a stock control system. Every time an item is sold, the record of number in stock is reduced by one. The system can keep track of what needs to be re-ordered. It allows the shop to do 'just in time' ordering. This is an advantage to everyone because:

- the shelves should never become empty
- the shop does not hold lots of unsold stock
- stock is fresher
- money stays in the shop's account for longer

Shopping for food has never been cheaper or offered so much variety and convenience. This is largely due to supermarkets taking full advantage of IT.

Progress check

1. Fill in the gaps.

   EFTPOS systems help shops to keep profitable because they allow .... ordering which helps to keep shelves full and stock fresh. As well as paying for goods, EFTPOS terminals allow the customer to receive .... using a debit card. .... bills let the customer check prices later.

2. Give two benefits of loyalty cards to:

   a) the customer
   b) the shop

3. Give two benefits of EPOS systems to:

   a) the customer
   b) the shop

4. Explain how stock control systems benefit from being linked to an EPOS system.

5. How does EFTPOS help cash flow in a supermarket?

Banking is generally convenient and trouble-free because the banks have had the enterprise to keep at the forefront of IT developments.

Statements

One of the earliest uses of computers in banks was to keep track of customer accounts and to print statements. This is a natural use of computers because it involves:

- huge amounts of data
- repetitious processes
- a need for accuracy
- speed

Cheque processing

Cheques have numbers on them, printed in MICR characters. They include the branch sort code, the account number and the cheque number. This allows customers' accounts to be updated automatically.

Direct debits

Direct debits allow a flexible sum to be deducted at intervals and make sure that bills don't get forgotten. Examples are:

- satellite TV bills
- mobile phone bills
- electricity payments
- credit card bills

Credit cards

Credit cards allow spending without cash by borrowing money from the credit card company and paying back all or some of the debt each month.

Debit cards

An example of a debit card is Switch. These cards let you pay for goods and services by drawing money that you already have from your bank account. They allow cash back services in supermarkets.

The cashless society

Cash is used less and less, but it will probably always be needed for small transactions and paying small businesses that do not have the right equipment for taking card payments. Some people prefer to use cash rather than run the risk of getting into debt.

Card security

Card details have been stored on a magnetic strip in the past. This is easy to clone, so more cards are equipped with smart chips that hold more data and are less easy to copy.

ATMs

ATMs (Automatic Teller Machines) – cash machines would not be possible without computer systems. They are needed to:

- connect the machines to the bank's databases
- check credit levels
- adjust account details
- provide balance enquiries
- connect different bank systems together

Telephone banking

Call centres can administer a bank account because of access to interconnected computer systems. Most transactions can be done over the telephone, but security is an issue and several passwords are sometimes needed to gain access to an account.

Online banking

With online banking you can:

- see a statement
- transfer money between accounts
- pay bills
- set up standing orders or direct debits

Again, security is an important issue as some customers have been tricked into giving their details away.

Progress check

1. What is an ATM?

2. How does an ATM rely on computer systems?

3. What is the difference between a credit card and a debit card?

4. What information is encoded on the bottom of cheques?

5. Why will the cashless society probably never happen?

6. State two services that are available from online banking.

Health and safety is a big issue these days. Employers have to guard against the smallest risk to their employees to avoid being sued. Many law firms make a good living by seeking to blame people and organisations for what used to be regarded as accidents.

The use of computers has its own special set of risks and difficulties.

RSI

Joints can get worn and muscles strained if they are used over and over to do the same activity. Extensive typing is a good example of this and can result in RSI (repetitive strain injury).

Remedy: take frequent breaks, use ergonomic keyboard, use voice-activated software, use wrist rests.

Backache

Backache can be caused by long periods of sitting, especially in uncomfortable chairs.

Remedy: get up frequently, choose a well-designed chair, adjust the chair to the correct and comfortable height.

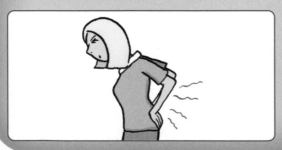

Eye strain

Eye strain can be caused by long periods of looking at a screen, with back lighting behind the screen.

Remedy: use larger screens, don't position screens in front of windows, use anti-glare filters.

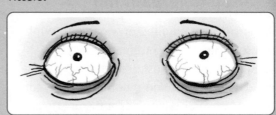

Stress

Stress can be caused by frequent changes in work patterns, new software and procedures to learn and trying to keep up to date.

Remedy: retrain when possible, say no to extra work, don't work long hours, don't take work home.

Physical dangers

Examples of physical dangers include: tripping over wires, electric shocks, lifting heavy equipment.

Remedy: wires should be enclosed in proper ducting, all live parts should be enclosed.

Disposal issues

Computers are not kept for ever. Eventually they have to be disposed of. Available landfill sites are on the decline and computers contain plastics that release toxic fumes when burned.

Remedy: charge manufacturers for proper disposal, recycle as much as possible, donate computers to less affluent users (although that only delays the disposal problem).

Public safety

Many safety-critical systems are run by computers: planes fly on autopilot for much of their journeys, computers are used in air traffic control, computers control railway signalling. Usually these work well, but there have been problems.

Remedy: commission good systems in the first place, not necessarily the cheapest, have backup systems in place, have human backup ready in case of problems.

Progress check

1 What is RSI and what causes it?

2 How can eye strain be avoided when using a computer?

3 How should computer users avoid backache?

4 Give two ways that computer systems can be a health and safety risk in an office.

5 Give one example of how a computer failure could endanger the public.

The Data Protection Act

The DPA was originally passed in the UK in 1984 and revised in 1998. Most other countries have similar laws. It concerns **personal data**.

> **Personal data is data about living individuals.**

The UK Data Protection Act defines certain individuals and principles.

Data controller

A data controller is a person who is responsible for the collection and use of personal data. The data controller is required to notify the Information Commissioner's office of intended use of personal data.

The Information Commissioner's Office

This government office keeps records of data controllers to ensure that they comply with the data protection principles.

The data subject

The data subject is the person about whom personal data is held. This person has rights to see the data.

The principles of the Data Protection Act

- Data should be fairly and lawfully processed.
- Data must be used only for the purposes specified in the register.
- Data should be adequate, relevant and not excessive.
- Data should be accurate and kept up to date.
- Data should not be kept for longer than necessary.
- Data should be processed only in line with the rights of the data subject.
- Data should be kept securely.
- Data should not be passed to countries that do not have adequate data protection legislation.

There are exemptions from the Data Protection Act for certain security, police and medical situations.

Computer systems are prone to abuse like anything else. You need to be able to categorise possible abuses and clearly relate these to legislation.

15 MINS

Computer abuse

Computer abuse covers many things that are regarded as unacceptable. However, the international nature of the Internet may cause legal difficulties when the source is not clear. Computer abuse includes:

- spreading spam
- spreading viruses
- posting of undesirable materials on websites
- cyberstalking, where people are harassed by repeated unwanted emails or chat messages
- fraud

Computer Misuse Act 1990

This UK Act was mainly designed to deter hacking. It forbids the unauthorised access of computer systems and files as well as altering them.

Much hacking is made possible by the careless use of passwords, but some determined hackers are talented programmers who break into systems just to prove that they can do it.

The Act also makes the creation and spreading of viruses an offence.

Progress check

1. State two rights that individuals have under the Data Protection Act.

2. Define:
   a) the Information Commissioner's Office
   b) a data subject
   c) a data controller

3. Which of these actions is forbidden by the Data Protection Act?
   a) passing data to a non-European Union country
   b) passing data to another company
   c) obtaining data by deception
   d) using personal data for statistical purposes
   e) using personal data for accounting purposes
   f) keeping data insecurely

4. What UK legislation is aimed at deterring hackers?

5. Give two examples of computer abuse.

COMPUTERS AND WORK

Few jobs do not involve using computers. Jobs have changed a lot over the years since computers were invented.

New jobs

Lots of jobs exist now that are specifically concerned with computers. Examples are: programmer, database administrator, systems manager.

More will be looked at on pages 88–89.

New industries have also been created as the result of computers, but do not necessarily focus on computers.

- The whole **mobile phone** industry could not have developed without computers.
- **Digital TV** depends on computer technology.

Changed jobs

Most jobs have changed as a result of computers. For example:

- **reporters** type their stories with word processors
- **doctors** keep computer records about patients
- **car mechanics** use engine diagnostic software
- **architects** use CAD
- **delivery drivers** use transmitters to record parcel delivery

Lost jobs

Some jobs have disappeared as a result of computer technology. For example:

- **typesetters** – books and newspapers are now produced by DTP software so there is no need for the typesetters who worked with hot metal to produce printed material
- **paint sprayers** – most cars are now painted by robots controlled by computer

Training

Computer systems change quite regularly. To succeed in work these days, it is necessary to retrain regularly or otherwise keep up to date. This can be expensive and stressful.

People change jobs more often than they used to. Fewer people look on a career as a choice for life any more.

Codes of practice

A code of practice could, for example:

- limit personal use of the Internet to lunch hours
- prohibit the use of company email for private purposes

Computers are used in most workplaces. You should be aware of ways in which jobs have changed as a result.

- prohibit the use of floppy disks
- prohibit the downloading of computer programs

Teleworking

ICT has made it possible for more people to work from home. This **teleworking** can make use of computers, email, Internet resources, direct connection to a company's network and video conferencing.

Teleworking **benefits the teleworker**:

- There's no need for commuting, so saving time, stress and money.
- Work can be done at a time to suit the teleworker.
- There's less involvement in office politics.
- It doesn't matter where you live.

Teleworking **benefits the employer**:

- Office space can be reduced.
- Teleworkers can be more productive.

However, there are **disadvantages**:

- family distractions
- a feeling that you are always at work
- missing out on office gossip
- loneliness

Often a halfway solution is a good idea, where workers spend some time at home and go to the office once or twice a week.

Progress check

1. Give two advantages of working from home.

2. Give two disadvantages of working from home.

3. Suggest two ways that a teacher might use ICT in his work.

4. Suggest two ways that a dentist might use ICT in his work.

5. State two items of hardware that a teleworker might need to work from home.

6. Why might a company introduce a code of practice concerning computer use?

Privacy

The widespread holding of personal data on computer systems makes privacy more unlikely. Laws such as the Data Protection Act are designed to protect the rights of individuals to privacy.

Your name and address

If you are a voter, this is held on the electoral register. Now it is possible to obtain these details online.

Your movements

- As you travel around, your mobile phone registers at each base station it is near. Your phone provider can thus track your movements.

- If you use a credit or debit card, there are records of where you made purchases.

- Your car registration can be photographed and the details looked up on the DVLA computer. If you drive in London, your car will be photographed many times.

Your purchases

- Loyalty cards can associate you with all your purchases at a particular shop or group of shops.

- There are records of all big purchases with insurance companies, credit companies and banks.

Police records

Police forces have computer records of people. One day they will probably have DNA records of everyone as well. In some countries, it is possible to look up the police records of anyone.

15 MINS

Intellectual property

When someone writes a book, a song, a computer program, the product is considered to be **intellectual property**. People have the right to be fairly rewarded for their creative efforts and those who use these products should pay a fair price for them.

Most copyright material is available digitally. It is easy to make perfect copies of music, movies, books and articles.

Infringement of copyright is likely to:

- discourage creative effort
- damage the music industry
- reduce the availability of new music

Plagiarism

Plagiarism is using someone else's work and pretending it is your own. It is a particular problem with student assignments, because it is so easy to copy and paste from websites. Plagiarism can lead to:

- legal problems for the student
- penalties, such as not being awarded a grade in an exam
- bad reputations for students and schools
- a tendency to avoid doing original work

Progress check

1. What is intellectual property?

2. Give two examples of how someone's movements can be traced by ICT methods.

3. What is a software licence?

4. What is plagiarism?

5. Give two problems that can be caused by plagiarism.

6. Explain why computer technology has made infringement of copyright more common than it used to be.

DAY 7

JOBS IN IT

It was once thought that computers would lead to widespread redundancies as they took over people's jobs. In fact, they have created more jobs. The variety of jobs in the IT industry is extremely wide.

Programmers

Programmers write the code that makes software work. There is always the need for more software, so there is always a need for programmers. They maintain existing systems too.

Systems managers

All organisations of any size have computer systems. They need to be managed and planned. Systems managers work with finance directors in deciding what new systems are needed. They make sure the different systems in an organisation work together.

Technicians

Technicians do the work of trouble-shooting and repairing computer systems.

Project managers

Most IT projects are carried out by lots of people. Project managers make sure that projects are finished on time and within budget.

Testers

Usually systems are tested by people other than those who created them. This is so that they are motivated to find errors.

Technical authors

Technical authors write the documentation for systems. They need to have technical expertise as well as the ability to write well.

Web developers

There is plenty of development work as websites continue to increase in number. Web developers often need database and programming skills.

Database administrators

The data of an organisation is sometimes in the charge of a specialist database administrator.

Network designers and installers

Most organisations have networks. Network design and the installation of networks is a specialist skill.

Hardware builders

Someone has to make the computers. This is mostly done by a few large companies, but some small manufacturers exist who give a personal service.

Systems analysts

Systems analysts advise and plan IT solutions.

Journalists

There are lots of computer magazines that always need articles. Some journalists specialise in articles about the IT industry and developments within the industry.

Writers

For each new IT course that is developed, textbooks are written, often by teachers of IT, who may also have experience in the examination and assessment process.

Progress check

1. Why is the IT industry providing so much employment?

2. a) Who writes technical documentation?
    b) Give one other example of a job in IT that involves writing.

3. Who decides on new IT systems in an organisation?

4. Who is consulted by a company that is planning a new computer system?

5. Which people might be involved in the planning and installation of a network?

6. Who makes sure that a project is finished on time?

ANSWERS

Computer systems
1. b, d, e
2. embedded system
3. a computer system that only has one specific purpose
4. data, information, program

Types of computer
1. accounts, letters, Internet, shopping
2. recordkeeping, computer-aided learning, data logging experiments, teaching IT
3. personal digital assistant (small hand-held computer)
4. terminal
5. desktop PC has separate processor unit, monitor and keyboard; laptop PC is portable
6. to control shutter speed, iris diaphragm, various control and display options

Storage media
1. smart card
2. storing multimedia presentations, distributing software, backing up
3. DVDs
4. CDs
5. backups, moving data

Parts of a computer system
1. hardware
2. operating systems and applications
3. buses
4. instructions
5. peripheral
6. ROM
7. modem
8. reduces

The processor and memory
1. data, instructions, any example of a program, data on its way in or out of the computer
2. RAM
3. to store settings and start-up routines, to store instructions in embedded systems
4. run instructions, perform arithmetic, compare values

5. 1 (an output signal)
6. 0 (no output)

Computer input
1. a) sensor
   b) flow sensor
   c) keyboard
   d) mouse
2. analogue-digital converter
3. magnetic ink character recognition – a system for encoding numbers on cheques
4. changes made by pen are not read
5. OMR
6. barcodes

Computer output
1. laser
2. they make carbon copies
3. screen/VDU
4. plotter
5. TFT/LCD
6. heaters, motors (on windows)

Storage devices and media
1. formatted
2. tracks
3. sectors
4. random access/direct access
5. file allocation table (FAT)
6. laser
7. fragmented
8. disk pack

Networks
1. bus
2. shared files, shared peripherals, shared software, communication
3. unauthorised viewing/privacy issues
4. upgrades, maintenance, technical support
5. network interface card (NIC)

Operating systems
1. graphical user interface (GUI)
2. disk formatter, defragmenter, text editor, picture editor, scandisk

3   driver
4   password protect, allow only certain users access
5   allows more than one program to be in a running state at the same time

Applications and database management systems

1   a)   operating system
     b)   application
     c)   application
     d)   application
     e)   operating system
     f)   operating system
     g)   application
2   database is a store of data, database management system is software that works on the data

Spreadsheets

1   a)   anything from A1 to F1 or A1 to B5
     b)   anything from C2 to F5
     c)   F2 to F5
2   D1 to E1 or F3 to F5
3   A2 to F5
4   =AVERAGE(C2:C5)
5   copy right/fill right

Modelling

1   a model is a set of mathematical relationships, a simulation is a representation of reality based on a model
2   in the future/unknown, factors, information
3   dangerous
4   slow

Desk top publishing

1   word processed
2   digital camera, scanned, drawn in art package, obtained as clip art, copied from another file
3   designed for page layout
4   desktop area, master pages, rotation of images
5   a page whose contents appear on every other page
6   a layout upon which a document is based
7   a container on a page for text or graphics

Word processing

1   cut, paste, search, replace, style
2   examples: there instead of their, to instead of two, told instead of tolled
3   any name, foreign word, unusual word
4   report produced in word processor, details such as name/comment merged from database
5   highlight text to change, change background colour for reduced eye strain, red underline for errors

Data logging and control

1   pH, magnetic, temperature, movement, pressure, proximity
2   a physical change leads to an effect which automatically reverses it
3   These are approximate.
     a)   logging period: 30 mins, logging interval: 1 minute
     b)   period: 1 week, logging interval: 1–5 minutes
     c)   logging period: 1 year, logging interval: 1 hour
     d)   logging period: 1 millisecond, logging interval: much less than 1 millisecond
     e)   logging period: days or weeks, logging interval: tenth of a second
4   a)   sensor: pressure pad/induction loop, actuator: light/switch
     b)   sensor: altimeter/pressure sensor, actuator: flaps/engines
     c)   sensor: light cell, actuator: motor

Miscellaneous software

1   knowledge base, inference engine, interface
2   images of windows, roof types, doors, bricks
3   presentations, Internet, CDs, interactive learning packages, data logging etc.
4   CAD is for making designs, CAM is for putting these designs into operation
5   computerised axial tomography (a way of making an image of the inside of someone's body)
6   it asks questions

Bits and bytes
1. as text, numbers, instructions, pixels, sounds
2. ASCII, EBCDIC, unicode
3. 2,097,152
4. pictures are often large files
5. one bit

Data types and databases
1. yes/no (boolean)
2. text
3. a table
4. flat file
5. to avoid inconsistencies

Files, tables, fields and records
1. a table
2. a record
3. a part of a record
4. easier to process, easier to find data, can predict the size of file
5. less wasted space, software independent
6. comma separated value (a standard for variable length files)
7. a unique identifying field
8. registration number
9. something about which data is stored
10. a named store on a disk or tape

Accuracy: validation and verification
1. on data entry
2. by verification
3. validation (type check)
4. an extra bit added to data to reduce the number of errors caused by corruption
5. c
6. in case of input errors, (double entry) verification
7. length check, type check, format/picture check

Searching databases
1. AND
2. select the fields such as name, age, set criteria to be >=20 AND <=30
3. an index

4. which table, which fields, what conditions
5. show all the red Peugeots

File handling
1. transaction file
2. master file
3. chronological
4. key field (or possibly alphabetical)
5. a new file created from transaction file and old master file

File access methods
1. serial
2. random (direct) access
3. with an index
4. has no particular structure/depends on the software that put it there
5. disk
6. sequential

Identifying and investigating problems
1. the client
2. systems analyst
3. observation, questionnaire, interview, focus group
4. accuracy important, lots of data, repetitive, speed important, quality important
5. those who work on it later will understand it
6. identification, analysis, feasibility study, design, implementation, testing, evaluation, production

Analysing systems
1.
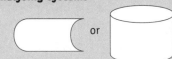
2. a verb
3. to show the planned solution to the client
4. when data is unintentionally changed after it has been stored
5. virus protection, parity checks, keep backups
6. include validation
7. easier to work on, can divide project up, give different parts to specialists, easier to test

Designing systems
1. to give instructions to the programmers
2. intuitive, clear colours, easy to navigate
3. check with the client
4. the fields to include, the data types, the field sizes
5. to speed up access
6. a report

Implementation and testing
1. trying out part of a solution before implementing the whole project
2. one that uncovers errors
3. test number, test data, expected result, actual result, action taken, part of system tested
4. a description of a database
5. to speed up project development, to make use of different expertise
6. alpha is carried out by the developers, beta is carried out by selected users

System documentation
1. a) program source code, test data, test results
   b) file locations, system requirements
   c) how to use, how to save, how to open files, FAQs, troubleshooting, error messages, tutorial
2. a) light, portable, easy to replace/copy
   b) easy to update, can collect data from users
   c) can read it anywhere
3. so that the installation can be rolled back if a problem occurs
4. software installed wrongly, in wrong place, wrong options installed
5. a work-through of the software with made-up examples

Evaluation and maintenance
1. the standards by which a project is judged
2. the client
3. fixing errors, if some errors have survived testing
4. incompatible with old data, with operating system or with hardware, undiscovered errors, insufficient training
5. support, maintenance, training, upgrades

The Internet
1. a set of rules that govern data transmission
2. examples: TCP/IP, FTP, HTTP, SMP, POP
3. an address of a resource on the Internet
4. computers/networks, telecommunication, World Wide Web, email, file transfer
5. image files are often large, they take longer to download than most word processed files

Email
1. a) quicker to deliver, cheaper, time zones don't matter
   b) don't have to wait for person, time zones don't matter
2. wastes bandwidth, wastes time in deleting it
3. advantage: can access it anywhere, can be free disadvantage: can be slow, limited storage, limited file attachments, prone to spam
4. a) carbon copy (send message to someone extra)
   b) blind carbon copy (does not reveal other addresses to copied recipient
5. confirms a live email address so you will get more

Ecommerce
1. ordering, advertising, email, teleconferencing
2. can order from anywhere, can shop around, save money, more choice, no need to travel
3. busy people, disabled people
4. wider choice, cheaper
5. less office space to pay for, can locate in cheap areas
6. bigger market, can introduce new activities/products

ICT and shopping
1. automatic, cash back, itemised
2. a) money off, special offers
   b) information about customer habits, customers return to collect more points
3. a) itemised bills, fresher goods, better stock levels, quicker service
   b) faster throughput, more customers served, fewer staff, can link to stock control

4 stock levels reduced as soon as purchase made
5 shop gets money immediately, less need to borrow

Banking
1 automatic teller machine/cash machine
2 checks ID/PIN/credit available, adjusts balances
3 credit card is for borrowing, debit card draws money you already have
4 bank sort code, cheque number, account number (later, the amount)
5 some traders won't have the equipment, people like to use cash for small transactions
6 balance enquiries, set up/change standing orders/direct debits, make payments

Health and safety
1 repetitive strain injury which is caused by carrying out the same action repeatedly
2 anti-glare screen, site screen away from windows, good lighting, good choice of screen colours
3 comfortable chair, sit properly, good angle between head and screen, take breaks
4 tripping over wires, fire hazards
5 air safety such as air traffic control issues, running nuclear power stations, etc.

Computer misuse and the law
1 to view the data that is held, to know that data is held securely and not passed on improperly
2 a) the person who registers data controllers
   b) someone about whom personal data is stored
   c) a person who is responsible for the storage of personal data
3 c, f
4 Computer Misuse Act
5 spreading viruses, cyberstalking, spreading offensive material

Computers and work
1 work at times to suit, can live anywhere, less travel
2 distractions, loneliness, out of touch
3 presentations, record keeping
4 storing patient details, Internet research, accounting
5 computer, modem/router, connection to computer's network
6 to reduce misunderstandings, to reduce computer misuse

Privacy and copyright
1 a creation of the mind to which the creator has financial rights
2 mobile phone, credit cards
3 permission to use software
4 pretending that someone else's work is your own
5 financial loss to the author, less likely that new creative work will be published, penalties for the plagiarist
6 easy to make quick and accurate copies of many types of file

Jobs in IT
1 it keeps changing, new uses continually being found
2 a) technical author
   b) journalist, book writer
3 systems manager
4 systems analyst
5 systems manager, network engineer, finance director
6 project manager

NOTES